What You Take To Heaven

Michael Harold Brown

Spirit Daily Publishing
www.spiritdaily.com
11 Walter Place
Palm Coast, Florida 32164

The publisher recognizes and accepts that the final authority regarding the apparitions in the Catholic Church rests with the Holy See of Rome, to whose judgment we willingly submit.

—*The Publisher*

What You Take to Heaven by Michael Harold Brown

Published by Spirit Daily Publishing

For additional copies, write:
Spirit Daily Publishing
11 Walter Place
Palm Coast, Florida 32164

or contact: www.spiritdaily.com

ISBN 978-0-692-28685-2

Printed in the United States of America

First Edition

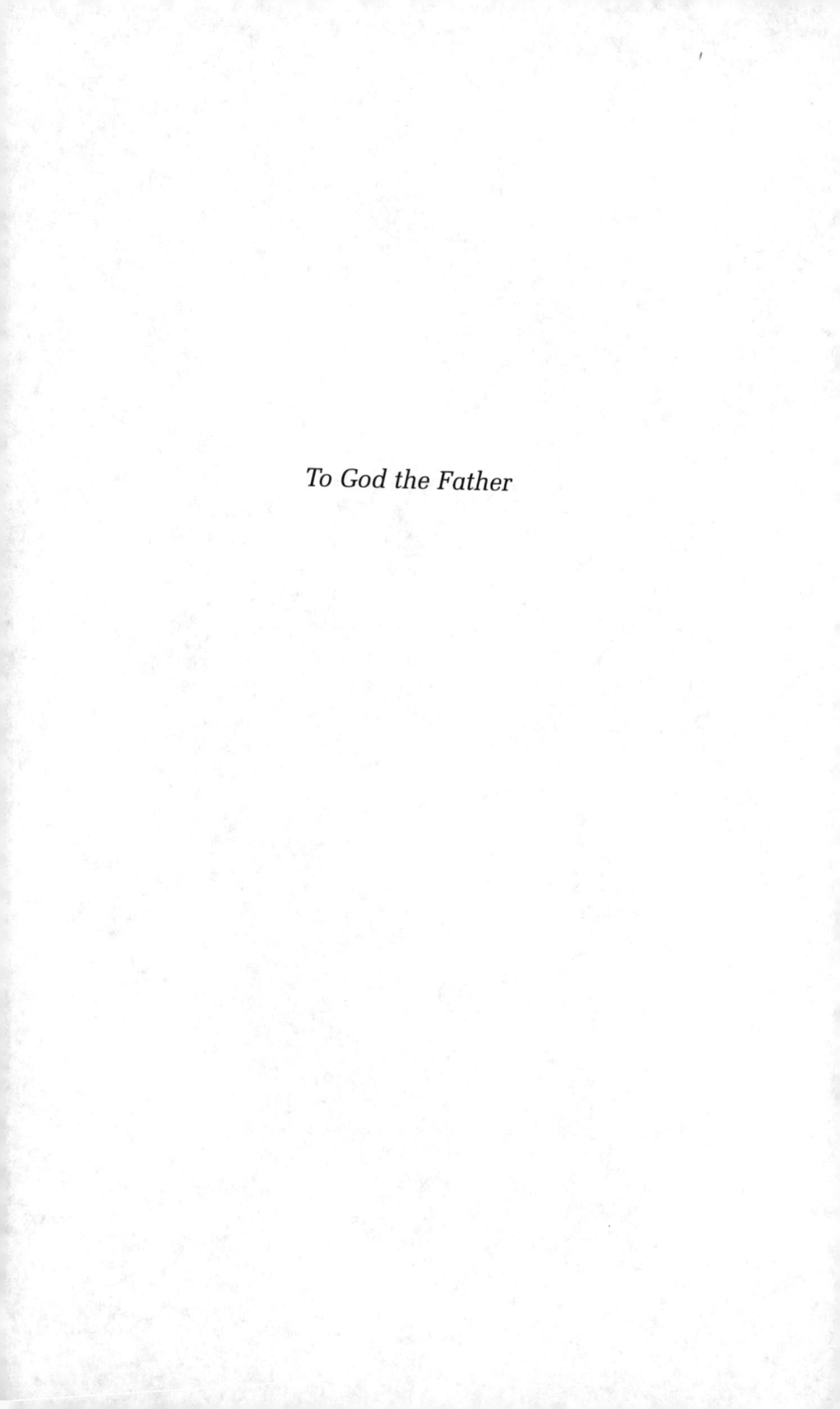

To God the Father

"Praise the Lord! Praise God in His sanctuary; praise Him in His mighty firmament! Praise Him for His mighty deeds; praise Him according to His exceeding greatness! Praise Him with trumpet sound; praise Him with timbrel and dance; praise Him with strings and pipe! Praise Him with sounding cymbals; praise Him with loud clashing cymbals! Let everything that breathes praise the Lord! Praise the Lord!" (Psalm *150)*

Chapter 1

When we die we will all be surprised.

No matter what you expect, and how big you expect it, how different, how phenomenal you anticipate the afterlife to be, you are going to be surprised.

For a good number, it will be the greatest surprise, the greatest joy, the greatest relief of our lives.

After reading dozens upon dozens of books about near-death experiences, interviewing those who've had them, studying what nurses, doctors, and surgeons have to say, speaking with folks who have a variety of mystical experiences (apparitions, glimpses of the other side), and having seen the incredible consistencies—the *overwhelming* consistencies—in these descriptions (whether Catholic, Protestant, Jewish, Buddhist, Hindu, Muslim, or for that matter agnostics and even atheists), and having spent decades now investigation supernatural phenomena, including apparitions of the Blessed Mother, visitations from departed souls, and such things as miraculous healings, I have no doubt about the supernatural.

None. None whatsoever.

We live forever.

That reality alone, just finally seeing it, will be surprise enough—eternity, before us, suddenly in great splendor.

Take the most iridescent, lush, and scenic landscape you have ever witnessed: compared to what you will see on the other side, it will be all but forgettable.

No matter how strongly you believe in it, the afterlife will be far larger and more splendiferous than you ever fathomed.

We have eternity to look forward to! And it's so vast it will *take* eternity to explore.

Even if I were writing as a skeptical, secular journalist, so compelling and consistent is the information from those who have died and come back that I would long ago have cast aside that skepticism.

There is overwhelming evidence, and it is so consistent that only a "diehard" would remain a doubter.

Final proof?

There is no final proof, not while we're on earth; not in the way that the world demands proof.

You cannot put God in a microscope (or telescope).

Faith is a big part of the test of life.

But the information, the testimonies, overwhelm those who look at it closely.

For me it is a fact: We live forever and when we die the great emotion, the *consuming* emotion, will be love, bliss, and astonishment. We will be in a place we cannot possibly visualize.

We'll be surprised. We'll be amazed. We'll be enthralled by our surroundings. We'll be amazed at who we really are. Everything will unfold as a wonder. There will be release. There will be a new existence. It will unfold in a way that is far past human design. There will be a freedom beyond what we have ever felt, and a sensation, an experience, of sudden, huge understanding. The wisdom of all ages will be infused in you instantly. Suddenly, everything will make sense—loved ones, birth, the struggles on earth, death, with the realization that you are where you actually belong. "I'm home," you'll think, on seeing Heaven. "I'm really here. *This* is my home." There will be—in Heaven—a sense of total well-being.

All will feel right there.

All will *be* right there. You will enter a realm (actually, realms plural) you never imagined and never could imagine.

In our time, everyone uses and overuses the term "awesome."

This will be *awesome*.

It will be beyond mesmerizing.

Think of the most incredible vista you have ever seen on earth, the Rockies as the sun rises, or an island off New Zealand, or a crystal-clear cool Florida spring, or sunset in Hawaii, or the African savannah, and know that any such vista will pale in comparison.

The greatest beauty on earth is a dull photographic negative.

On earth, everything's illuminated from exterior sources (the sun, fire, or electricity). Over "there"—past the threshold, through the passage—all will be illuminated from the interior; all will have a source of light; light will suffuse you; everything will be alive in praise for God.

I have written about the "other side" before.

But I'd like to take it from a new perspective.

I'd like to take it from the perspective of eternity, and what we bring there—who we will be, what we will be, where we will be.

We live forever. Even those who are "believers"—including devout ones—have trouble realizing it. We can pray and attend Mass or Adoration and say the Rosary and visit places like Fatima or Israel and still harbor doubts about the afterlife.

This is a test of life, a suffering. While we're here, on earth, we wear "blinders." There is a limit—what I call a "cap"—on our perception, our intellect, and our understanding. Often, little makes sense. There are "disconnects" (breaks or knots) in our lives. It's like looking at a work of tapestry from the bottom: we get only a general idea of what's atop, on the other side, what the final work will look like; we see just threads that seem to go nowhere. It can even be unsightly—as life so often is!

When we view it from the other side, however—from above (where we see the finished product)—everything will be connected into a design of unblemished beauty.

It will all make sense.

With surprise, we will think or exclaim:

"Now I see. Oh, if only I'd known. That's incredible. That's wonderful. I had no clue!"

"I should have known," you may murmur—or shout.

We will begin to see that God is perfect and that He wasted not a moment—a split second—of our lives on earth. Everything counts. Everything's connected. He's not a God Who winds up clocks and then lets them go off on their own.

He knows the minutes of our lives, *every second*. He is involved with every "tick" of the clock. He certainly knows when our time runs out! Sometimes, He sets an alarm for us. He pushes us through events (back onto the right track). Mostly, He whispers to the intuition through His angels and Holy Spirit and here is another surprise:

When we die, we will meet our guardians. With eyes wide open we will see the presences we have felt around us through our lives. They will seem older and closer than dearest friends. They *are* older and more dear than any friend. We will be surprised when we see them and yet it will also be like a reunion. They will look exactly as we should have expected them to look. We'll learn they were far more important than we thought. We will be astounded—awed—at how many times they orchestrated events—had designed our meeting people who became important to us (such as a spouse), had inspired us, had kept us from danger, had stood by in special numbers at crucial moments such as the birth of a child or during Holy Mass. We will in many cases find out that there was more than one.

When we "pass," we'll see that there were more spirits, in most cases, in most places, on earth—demons, disembodied souls, purgatorial spirits, angels, saints, the Blessed Mother, the Lord Himself— than beings of flesh and blood. We'll see that we are immersed in a spiritual dynamic that most people (due to skepticism) rarely glimpse. We will see angels clothed in what seem like tiny sparkling lights that are ephemeral and yet somehow more real than what is physical; woven threads of light.

This is the supernatural reality.

We see just fleeting snippets of it.

Nothing will have a blemish.

Right now, the supernatural is fleeting to us. We may sense it in a dream that comes true, in a knowing what someone is thinking, in correctly guessing that a long-lost friend is on the phone. It can be a mother's "intuition." It can be knowing another is in trouble. It can be a sudden inspiration. It can be a vague voice, a calling in the wake-dream state, a strange knock, the glimpse of a light (or shadow); a speck of luminosity; an apparition or vision or perhaps the dream of loved ones in a place that is unlike here.

When we die, we'll be surprised at how many relatives we have—will eventually meet all our ancestors going back to the beginning of time, be reunited with friends, be amazed that they and everyone else know all about us—that there are no secrets—and yet will carry no embarrassment with us. *Everyone will understand everyone (mind to mind) and in an instant will see who others truly are.*

What is inside will now be on the outside.

The pure white robes we wear will reflect inner purity.

Around us, there will be meadows and valleys and mountains and grass and hedges and trees and flowers and fruit and plants that bear no resemblance to anything on earth. There will be ponds, lakes, and streams. There will be "living waters" that are released by a "sea of fountains": every droplet of which emits its melody and tone, intermingling with choruses of ineffable music all around.

The flowers will be of no known colors and will make the most radiant red, the most splendid azure, the brightest gold on earth look like shadows.

There will be green meadows in the original essence and absolute fullness of that color.

There will be plants with huge white-petaled flowers and a gold center on the same vine as lush radiant purple grapes amid flowers of other types and alive in such a way that if you picked one, another would instantly take its place: grow spontaneously.

These are actual testimonies. God infuses all. There is His energy—the power of the universe—in every aspect of the environment. Think to the most beautiful day you have ever spent. Perhaps it was a Caribbean beach. Perhaps it was atop a mountain. Perhaps it was a perfect breeze on a perfect summer day in your own yard. Those sensations—a soothing breeze, on a day in the seventies, with no humidity—give us only the beginning, the very beginning, the tiniest idea, of the pleasant feelings that will surprise us in Heaven.

That will astound us.

Think about it this way: in Heaven there are no mistakes, no tension. No one argues. One receives immediate answers to all questions. You will simply have to think of it. In less than an instant, you're going to understand how big the universe is, how it was formed, how many other universes there are, the gulfs between firmaments, and—beyond those—how many dimensions there are. We'll see the nature of every single earthly cell and their relation with every other cell, how earth was created, when it was made, and the way life began (in all its forms). All you will have to do is wish to know anything—wish to go back and see how it was like in the days of cavemen, how it was on the ship with Columbus, or how many peoples lived in America before recorded history—and the answers will come like video.

Did early dinosaurs and humans co-exist?

How exactly was Israel in the time of Christ?

What did He actually look like?

And the Blessed Mother?

Joseph?

What other miracles did He perform (see *John* 21:25)?

You will gain access to every single mystery that has ever fascinated you. Talk about surprise! Each thing that ever caused you to wonder will now be revealed in a way that'll amaze you with its obviousness. *Now it all makes sense! Of course! I should have known.* And more than anything that thought, that surprising amazing thought: *I'm home!*

Chapter 2

Immediately the full scale and details of what was assigned to us—our missions on earth—will be shown. Surprised? You may be startled—fairly gasp at what your assignment was, or at least the full extent of it.

Do you understand what you were to do? Did you finish your task? What do you bring with you? How have you served God?

You will feel utter joy if you have completed your tasks, accomplishing what you were assigned to accomplish.

Reviewing those tasks, you will see the "big" in the small and the small in the big.

Christ and the angels will not care about many of those things that seem like such *big* deals to you on earth.

Many of those you will leave behind.

There are big things you do on earth that may also be big things in Heaven but often it will be those little things, those little touches, those little expressions of sacrifice, longsuffering, humility, and love, that will accompany you.

These are the treasures of Heaven (*Matthew* 6:20).

These are the matters that will count, along with your mission.

The totality of your love.

If you love, you will hear your heavenly name called. A heavenly name, a long one, awaits you—and will be spoken as if by the roar of a waterfall.

Once in Africa I met a visionary who said she had experienced the afterlife. This woman was from the apparition site of Kibeho that had been formally approved by the Church. During her experiences, the Rwandan, Anathalie Mukamaimpka, said she had been taken by the Blessed Mother on a "journey" to paradise and during the journey had been whisked to what she was told was *"Isangano"*—the "place of communion," which she also called the "highest part of Heaven." There, she said, seven exquisitely handsome men in brilliant pure-white cloaks were in a circle creating gorgeous music (though with no instruments), each note filled with a different sensation of contentment and joy (as one writer noted).

This occurred in 1982.

There was also a place where Anathalie saw "millions of people dressed in white." They were not quite as blissful as the seven men but still "overwhelmingly happy." This, she said, was *"Isenderezwa z'ibyishimo,"* or, the "place of the cherished of God."

Let's continue for a moment on what the higher parts of Heaven hold: buildings far more massive than any on earth, with no walls, at least not walls like we know walls, transparent yet fashioned with substances that bear resemblance to precious crystallized jewels—libraries larger than all the buildings in Washington D.C. put together and a meeting place for a council others have described as "wise men" who evaluate those who enter bedecked in that pure whiteness and dressed like monks and as full of wisdom as they are of love. "It was beautiful inside, with mahogany, and cherry wood, and—[words fail]; just beautiful," said one woman who was escorted by a group of men into a building. "We walked up a winding staircase which was similar to a courtroom . . . In the middle of the room was a large elongated oval table with chairs all around it. In the corner there was an enclosed area with a beautiful engraved fence. There was a platform behind the fence in sort of a closed circle. I was asked to stand there. The men went and sat around the table. They began to discuss whether or not I should be allowed to stay or go back."

Another found himself in a dazzling white building and entered to wait in an anteroom. "They said I was to remain here until some sort of disposition had been made in my case. Through wide doors I could glimpse two long tables with people sitting at them talking—about me." Sometimes, Jesus, who of course has ultimate say, reappears at these discussions.

Some trees will look like those on earth while others will be nothing like what we see on this planet, taller than skyscrapers, with branches that arch for miles, others minute; none will have a dead branch or leaf, all exuding the life force of our good and brilliant and endlessly kind Lord.

There will be the trees that are in perfect symmetry with bushes and gardens, along with the structures, which will seem more like works of art than buildings. A gorgeous hue will be emitted. They will be defined but not solid. There will be grass that seems to sway with the gorgeous chime-music that has a life all its own. Every movement will add to a song. "Light hit the side of the tunnel and burst into pastel colors that were alive and sparkling," one woman told me. "If they could have giggled, they would have—they were full of life. *Everything* there was full of life. Everything was at a vibrant peak of perfection. Heaven is full of life and all about life. And there were the bells, the birds, the music. There were lots of hills. No shadows. The sky was like sapphire azure blue and it was alive! I saw planets and stars—gee, I can't tell you, but when I see pictures like that, I'm 'home' in Heaven again! I heard the turning of the planets. An angel told me it was the harmony of harmonies, the symphony of symphonies. I can still hear them. You see: everything exists to praise God. Everything. We just can't hear it (here on earth). One time, after my experience, I was praying and looking out the window at the tree line. As the trees were gently swaying in the wind my eyes were opened to see liquid lines moving with the breeze upward toward God. The scripture came to mind: the trees of the field will clap their hands" (*Isaiah* 55:12).

In Heaven, in paradise, whatever the level, truth is translated into song.

And heals the spirit.

All of the earth's symphonies, said another, "pale in comparison."

"There was a sound in the air that completely defies description," added the woman I spoke with (who hailed from Michigan). "It was as if there were a multitude of voices and a multitude of instruments, blended and playing soft music. The twittering of birds and other beautiful sounds were all melodically instrumented into the music that wafted through the air."

"It sounds loud and piercing as a trumpet, yet the notes glide smoothly as a violin and also as sweetly pitched as a flute," noted the one who mentioned symphonies. "It is all these rich sounds blending perfectly as one. As I concentrated on the music, it gracefully slowed down to a soothing lullaby. The effect was the most beautiful and emotionally soothing song I have ever heard!"

Pure, soft music, with sanctity, is the air of paradise.

It's absorbed. It is digested. It vivifies. On earth, it affects us more than we know.

It is the resonance of the soul and in Heaven it is only a good, positive, and uplifting resonance.

Our spirits reverberate with God.

Think wind chimes.

"I found myself in a place of such beauty and peace," another woman recounted. "It was timeless and spaceless. I was aware of delicate and shifting hues of color with their accompanying 'rainbow' sounds."

"Exquisite harmonies."

"A celestial choir."

"Sublimely beautiful."

"Unearthly tones."

Those who return say it was like the gardens, the leaves, the colors were singing. Every drop of the living waters will emanate notes that coalesce with a perfect harmony of tones praising God—with all the sounds around.

"A thousand tiny golden bells."

"Make music, the heavenly blend of birds, voices, instruments, and bells, and you're there!" said the Michigan woman.

"It flowed unobtrusively, like a glassy river, quietly worshipful, excitingly edifying, and totally comforting," said a near-deather named Richard Eby.

"High sweet tones."

"I found myself saying, 'Bach is only the beginning!'" said Dr. George Ritchie, a psychiatrist who "died."

In a chorus, the whisper: "Jesus."

Indeed, high sweet tones!

Jesus, Jesus, Jesus.

Balm indeed!

We will be surprised how everything is in the *now*, that tomorrow is yesterday and today is also tomorrow.

On earth, our knowledge is "capped." How restricted we are! How liberated we will feel. Those who have the experience of glimpsing Heaven (and there are now *millions*) don't want to return to their bodies any more than you'd want to take a long warm bath and then put dirty clothes back on.

We'll be surprised to see that the spiritual realm is more real than the physical one!

Returning to earth, they tell us, is like being slammed back into a stark, hostile reality. (Some have even become angered at nurses and doctors or other medical personnel for reviving them!)

That's how great, how *surprisingly* pleasant, how endlessly delightful, eternity is! If we could all experience it, we would lose any fear. Death, as the Bible tells us, would lose its "sting." Those who have this experience do just that: they are no longer afraid of dying and in fact look forward to it (their death) but are also in no hurry for they realize now that every person on earth has a special assignment and they want to make certain they fulfill theirs.

On the other side, at the entrance to bucolic pastures, to lush meadows, the verdant horizon, below a cloudless "sky," with the company of angels (now visible!), flowers drip light. Stones will sparkle. All glistens. There'll be streets and walkways with crystal-gold paving stones. "After a little while I saw my daughter," noted an Englishwoman. "We were in a garden where the grass was so green and lush. The flowers were incredibly bright, and there were fruit trees. Someone picked an apple from one of the trees, and it immediately grew back again. Everyone there was totally whole, and my daughter was just wonderful. We talked about how much we loved each other, and how happy she was to see me. The feelings were mutual, but of a higher level than we understand on earth."

"Isenderezwa z'ibyishimo," the place of bliss, and once there, all will be seen in stereo, actually, we'll see all angles of everything, and everyone, at once—close or at a great

distance: it won't matter—to the extent that at first we may not even recognize our bodies (when looking back at what we left behind).

Take the colors from the prism of the most finely cut diamond and you begin (but only begin) to get a sense of the nature of what is formed on the other side. Think the deepest peace; total relaxation. This will be the constant state (and then some). Conceptualize your happiest moments and greatest thrills and multiply them by eternity. It is no exaggeration. It's not fantasy. If it seems like that—hyperbole, florid prose—it's because we struggle to describe what's beyond verbiage: the secret places, the halls, the purity and clarity; such absolute *clarity*! There are flowers with intense colors that might be compared to pebbles that have been polished in a pure, running stream, but they are not pebbles; they are more like rubies and pearls and sapphires, lit with exquisitely subtle neon as light streams from and around and through everything: the Light of life, which is love, which is the Light of God.

The fact that God even created us will be our source of greatest "thanks." It will be part of the surprise. You may ask: *How did I deserve this? How did I earn a place that is forever? How did I win the opportunity? How did I warrant His Love?*

Bring gratitude with you.

This is not a musing. It is not wishful thinking. It's based on reports that are now so widely reported (even by nurses, doctors, and surgeons) that they erase doubt.

God is so good that we can't imagine the extent of it.

Upon death, these are words to bring: *Jesus, Jesus, Jesus. God is good.*

Whatever your question, the one truth is that God is ultimate, inexhaustible, and unfathomable charity.

On the other side, every trauma on earth—even the most "horrendous"—will seem like nothing. No trial, no suffering, no discomfort will seem overwhelming. *They just won't.* (You will not take any misery unless you choose to!)

The longest life on earth (even those long-lived figures in the Old Testament) is just a flash. It truly is! And each moment must be treated like a pearl.

It *counts*.

And it never comes again.

God is perfect and wastes not a nanosecond. Even our thoughts bear weight. We'll take every single one of those with us (along with words and actions) and knowing this must ask: how could we neglect the way we face trials, how could we do, why would we *want* to do, anything that would detract from immediate entry into Heaven?

If this is on our minds every moment, with every prayer, every day, we have a good chance of making it to those higher reaches.

We all have that opportunity by virtue of the fact that everyone reading this is alive. There is still time—no matter what you have done (or failed to do). It's not too late. You just have to clean out the wrong stuff in your luggage now and bring the right stuff with you.

Truth is in that Light and we see ourselves in it as we truly are.

We see everything.

We see the very nature of life.

We begin to understand God.

We understand ourselves.

We see what we have brought there before embarking on the journey of a "lifetime."

Chapter 3

There is Heaven. There is purgatory. There is hell.

Before journeying, however, before knowing where we're headed (before we're "placed," which we'll get to), we must know *who we really are.*

Put it this way: the first person you meet in eternity will be yourself.

At the entrance to those gardens, on those roads, the first person you see will be the you that Jesus sees.

There will be no hiding who you are.

You will stand there in your full essence.

This should be exciting, something we look forward to (if we're prepared)!

You bring your true self, your total identity.

But it leads to a flurry of questions.

What defines you?

Where do you fit in with others?

What have you done in life (really *done*)?

What have you accomplished when you take a close look at your life?

Do you sense your role in God's Plan?

How do you treat and feel about others?

How much have you learned? Who and how much have you loved?

How much do you love God?

One day, you will see that there are no more important questions.

Don't panic if you feel you fall short, right now, in answering them.

God cares about where you are now.

Accept yourself and pursue life with vigor; follow your love. This will keep to your authentic self. Compassion will surround you—just surround you. The totality of your identity goes with you. As another noted, your true identity will be there, but in a greater way. As a researcher notes, "When we experience ourselves as the Light sees us, we will finally be free to experience ourselves as we really are." It is important to accept yourself and have compassion. Every time we exercise unconditional love, we advance. We purge. We elevate. There are new insights. We break fetters. Said a woman named Karen, "There is a God Who loves all of us—a forgiving God. The love that God feels for us, we should try to replicate in our feelings for others. Our purpose in being here is to learn what life presents us with and to overcome obstacles. Life is a training ground. As situations present themselves we should try to do the best we can, that's all He asks of us."

When it's time to review your life, it will be just that: a review. While, as we will see, there is a hell (for sure!), and limbo, those who are with Christ can be certain that a reliving of their lives will be a fascinating journey through life from a completely different, supernatural perspective.

Let's take a look at this idea of a life review.

And from who better than those who have experienced it?

"When the light appeared, the first thing said to me was, 'What do you have to show what you've done with your life?', or something to that effect," said a woman quoted in a groundbreaking book back in 1975. "And that's when these flashbacks started. I thought, 'Gee, what is going on?', because, all of a sudden, I was back early in my childhood. And from then on, it was like I was walking from the time of my very early life, on through each year of my life, right up to the present. It's not like he was trying to see what I had done—he knew already—but he was picking out these certain flashbacks of my life and putting them in front of me so that I would have to recall them. All through this, he kept stressing the importance of love. There wasn't any accusation in any of this, though. When he came across times when I had been selfish, the attitude was only that I had been learning from them, too. He seemed very interested in things concerning knowledge, also. He kept on pointing out things that had to do with learning, and he did say that I was going to continue learning, and he said that even when he comes back for me (because by this time he had told me that I was going back) that there will always be a quest for knowledge. He said that it is a continuous process, so I got the feeling that it goes on after death. I think that he was trying to teach me, as we went through those flashbacks. The whole thing was really odd. I was there; I was actually seeing these flashbacks; I was actually walking through them, and it was so fast. Yet, it was slow enough that I could take it all in."

Said Dr. Rene Turner of a glorious man she encountered, "He stood beside me and directed me to look to my left, where I was replaying my life's less complementary moments. I relived those moments and felt not only what I had done but also the hurt I had caused. Some of the things I would have never imagined could have caused pain. I was surprised that some things I may have worried about, like shoplifting a chocolate as a child, were not there, while casual remarks which caused hurt unknown to me at the time were counted. When I became burdened with guilt, I was directed to other events which gave joy to others, although I felt unworthy. It seemed the balance was in my favor. I received great love."

Another, Rita Bennett, in a book called *To Heaven and Back*, said, "As I lay there I relived every instance of my existence, every emotion and thought. I saw why I was the way I was; I re-experienced the way I had dealt with people and they with me. I saw where I could have done better. I felt emotions I was ashamed of, yet I realized there were things I had done well and felt good about. As we looked at different scenes, I would respond, 'Yes, I see how I could have done it another way, a better way.' I wondered how anyone could feel worthy in God's Presence. I wasn't condemned, but I didn't feel worthy. It's hard to explain. The whole time that was going on, for how long I don't know, I kept praising God. With the ending of my life review, I felt absolutely unworthy of being there in the Presence of this magnificent Light; unworthy in comparison to the grand scheme of things. It is all so beautiful, and what am I? I said this to God. Then Jesus' Hand touched me, and I was able to get back on my feet because I had previously had no strength. Taking me by the hand, He led me to the side of a main arena. He looked into my eyes, into my soul, and I knew He knew and understood everything I felt. When Jesus looked into me, it was with more love than I ever thought possible for anyone to know. He smiled, one look letting me know everything would be all right."

When we die, we see our entire lives, but with His Eyes.

We hear what we said, during life, with His Ears.

We feel with His understanding.

We will hear the thoughts that were behind our words.

Looking back, we'll see our bodies, there on a bed, at home, or at a hospital, on a gurney, wherever passage took place, and will no longer identify with it. Our physical self will be no more. We won't *want* it to be "us." If we pray enough (the Blessed Mother once promised), we will not even feel the passage at death. We'll be our minds. We will be our thoughts. This causes us to ask: *What flows through our minds in an average hour, what are our thought processes like, what do we think is important, what emotions flow most frequently? Is there hate? Dislike? Resentment? Unforgiveness? How often do we lust? Are we jealous? Is there greed? Are we worried that our pride will be "hurt"? What would be most wrenching to part with upon leaving this world? Who would be "too" wrenching to part with? Are we over-attached to anyone or anything? Who has helped us in life; what have we done to help those in need? Were there opportunities to help that we ignored? Are there any currently? How much of our lives are lived for Him? Do we pray from the soul (or by rote)? Is Jesus in our hearts—really there? Or do we just say He is?*

These and other questions are crucial to ask, here on earth, while we have time, for the first person you meet when you die will be your core self along with a deceased loved one or an angel—and Christ. In His Light, the truth, the whole truth, and nothing but the truth—about what we have done, where we've been, how we have made others feel, what we have learned (or failed to learn), and the essence of our lives will be shown in living color. Said a veteran who "died": "I could remember everything; everything was so vivid. It was so clear in front of me. It shot right by me from the earliest things I can remember right on up to the present. It was not anything bad at all. The best thing I can think of is to compare it to a series of pictures; like slides. It was just like someone was clicking off slides in front of me, very quickly."

Imagine seeing scenes from your life—in a stroller pushed by your parents, being fed early in life, coddled—that are not even in your earthly recollection.

You will hear your mom coo to you as an infant. You'll hear "Happy Birthday" when you were five. You'll walk across the stage at graduation again.

Every memory will be with you.

So will your effect on every person who crossed your path.

Even strangers.

They will be strangers no longer.

You'll know everything about everyone.

When we die, it will all look different—not just the reality of eternity but the reality from which we came—earth.

We'll be surprised at why what happened occurred.

We'll see why it did.

We'll be amazed at how our lives were designed.

We'll be astounded at hidden connections—and those long-lost memories.

We'll see the reasons for war, suffering, disease, disaster.

All will make sense.

Not one thing will make God seem harsh.

We will learn that there are no accidents.

We will see—and this is important—that there are no real tragedies on earth, but for spiritual ones, but for what sullies the spirit, but for bad choices of free will.

Hard things were corrections, were jolts, were stepping stones, were experiences of learning.

The injuries from any trauma, any "tragedy," will vanish without your even noticing it—*any* injury, any pain, even what was most hurtful, what was most excruciating, what was most severe, if, at death, you are willing to let it evaporate; if you have decided to forgive; if you leave it behind (where it belongs).

"The most surprising thing is what happened next," says the account of an evangelical pastor Daniel Ekechukwu, from Onitsha, Nigeria, who had an incredible experience while he was "dead" for two days (they had even begun to inject him with embalming fluid). The escorting angel told him, "If your record is to be called here, you will in no doubt be thrown into hell." Pastor Daniel immediately defended himself saying, "I am a man of God! I serve Him with all my heart!" But a Bible "immediately appeared in the angel's hand," notes the rendition of this experience, and it was opened to *Matthew* 5, in which "Jesus warned that if one calls his brother a fool he is guilty enough to go into the hell of fire (see *Matthew* 5:21-22). Pastor Daniel knew he was guilty for the angry words spoken to his wife. The angel also reminded him that Jesus promised that God will not forgive our sins if we do not forgive others (see *Matthew* 6:14-15) because we will reap what we have sown. Only those who are merciful will obtain mercy (*Matthew* 5:7). The angel told Daniel that the prayers he prayed as he was dying in the hospital were of no effect, because he refused to forgive his wife even when she attempted to reconcile on the morning of his fatal accident."

For our discernment.

The only tragedy is when something holds us from the best possible entry into Heaven. "Flash-brilliant colors came radiating from within me, to be displayed in front of me, like a theatre floating in the air," said a person who reported to the near-death institute in Seattle. "Everything I had ever said or done, or even thought, was right there, for all of us to experience. I rethought every thought, I re-experienced every feeling, as it happened, in an instant. And I also felt how my actions, or even just my thoughts, had affected others. When I had passed judgment on someone else, I would experience myself doing that. Then I would change places in perspective and experience what that judgment had felt like for them to receive from me. I'd return to my own feelings, to be able to respond to the drama I'd just witnessed and experienced, to react, for example, with shame or remorse because of that episode. Multitudinous actions or thoughts, derived from my own meanness, unkindness, or anger, caused me to feel the consequent pains of the other people. I experienced this even if at the time I had hurt someone, I had chosen to ignore how that would affect them. And I felt their pain for the full length of time they were affected by what I had done. Because I was in a different dimension where time can't be measured, as we know time to exist on earth, it was possible to know all of this and experience it all at once in a moment [a flash] and with the ability to comprehend all this information!"

"If you will let the fire of the Holy Spirit shoot through your being and make you pure, you will be able to walk boldly before God with a clean heart and a clear mind," said a man named Roberts Liardon who experienced death. "You will know you can walk into His Presence where you belong. As Jesus stepped back from me, it was as if He pulled down a large screen out of the air. On this screen, He began to show me my past life."

There is nothing more important than this notion:

When we die, each "little" and "large" aspect of what we lived will be reviewed, by Our Great Loving Lord, along with how we lived it.

"There was a reason for *everything* that happened, no matter how awful it seemed in the physical realm," said a woman named Beverly Brodsky, who "died" in a motorcycle crash in Los Angeles. "And within myself, as I was given the answer, my own awakening mind now responded in the same manner: 'Of course,' I would think, 'I already know that. How could I ever have forgotten!' In time the questions ceased, because I was suddenly filled with all the Being's Wisdom. I was given more than just the answers to my questions; all knowledge unfolded to me, like the instant blossoming of an infinite number of flowers all at once. I was filled with God's knowledge, and in that precious aspect of His Beingness, I was one with Him. My journey of discovery was just beginning."

Said a celestial being on the other side to a Romanian who was "dead" for twelve hours and encountered a massive tree with many kind of luminous colorful fruit, "Do you know what these trees represent? When we were people like you and based on how we received gifts on earth, that is how the eternal tree developed here. All people of the world receive gifts to serve God or the evil one." Added the Romanian, "People ask me, 'How do [folks] serve the evil one?' Through curses and swearing words, they are the prayers of the devil. I pray that all stay away from curses and swearing words."

Your entire life will pass before you, as on a television, maybe a hologram, maybe a rapid series of slides, a movie, perhaps on the pages of a celestial book (held by Jesus). However you see it, you will look at yourself from the perspective of how much goodness, kindness, and love you spread to others.

There will be thoughts. There will be incidents. There will be discussions. There will be compliments. There will be insults. There will be arguments. It will get to the bottom of the real you. Much you will have forgotten—chalked up as irrelevant. It may be a "three-D panoramic" view. It could be a Book of Life. Christ may hold it. An angel may hold it. It will answer those most fundamental questions of who you are, what's behind the face, what's behind your name, what's beneath who you fashioned yourself to be, why you were in the family you were, how you happened upon your friends, how circumstances were arranged such that you met your spouse, how much light is at the bottom of your soul, how much of a shadow, the beams of light.

Our spiritual eyes will see detail in a way that will astound us.

Answers will come to questions as soon as we think of them.

To move with that speed, we will have to have left all hurts, all failure, all disappointment, all injuries: physical, emotional, spiritual behind. We can't fit through the "narrow gate" with too much of the wrong luggage—nor the wrong language. In fact, we can't fit through with any. There are those who are so burdened with things of the earth that they literally go nowhere, endless accounts of those who either through fear, over-attachment, lack of knowledge, or bodily appetites refuse to go to the Light of Jesus (remaining on earth to continue their addictions, which can be food, drink, sex, or whatever).

Remember, there is still free will. There is *always* free will. It is a precious principle. And we exercise it when the physical realm ends. We bring our will with us and when we decide that God is to be shunned or feared, that we don't want to encounter Jesus, face to Face, we can slow our progress, to say the least. No doubt you have heard stories about how "ghosts," and spirits linger. They "haunt." They do not have clarity. They "passed" in a state of confusion. This makes it important that we have clarity of prayer and Confession. When we release the last bits of pride, selfishness, ego, dislike, resentment, and so on, matters become clearer to us. There is no longer clutter in front of our spiritual eyes. The state you "die into" may resemble—in clarity or murkiness, in peace or consternation, in light or dark—the state of mind you have put yourself in during your last moment. Those who die while on drugs often find themselves in a confused, spinning, fearsome state that goes beyond the dizziness caused by drugs. A confused person remains confused. Such a spirit may wander. It is in a condition some call the "place of bewildered souls." "I was terrified," said a man named Ray Kinman who died as a nine-year-old boy, tossed to the cement by a friend taking karate. "The feeling of fear began escalating, chaotic feelings. *'You're bad you're bad you're bad.'* I was terrified. I realized I'd gone crazy and said, 'well, if I'm crazy there's nothing I can do about it.' At that point I let go. I released the chaos. At that point, the pleasant sensations began, starting with peace and contentment. Then those feelings started amplifying, until it was just utter bliss, so beautiful! That's when I became aware of a little tiny point of Light. It was intense and brilliant, a zillion times brighter than the sun. I knew I had to go there. That's where the love was. The love was so intense you could touch it, you could roll around in it."

On earth, in prayer, through religion, we learn to abandon ourselves and head for the Light.

God speaks to us when we are humble and simple. Look at who He has chosen to be seers at places such as Fatima and Lourdes. The humble see the most. This is true also when we die. God really wants you to be simple. It is how He entered the world. Once we head for His Light, whether through a passage, or simply "flying" to Him, suddenly finding ourselves in His midst, we're shown what Heaven is like and loved ones who are there. We are taken on a little tour, up to a point. There is a boundary we can't pass. Perhaps it is beyond the boundary that we gravitate to where we need to go. The Romanian fellow, Gavril Barnut, a Communist, felt led by the devil initially and "automatically" saw a "dark world" and an evil spirit. The devil's body, he said, was "white but his hair was black with wire and his clothes red. It had a rough appearance, very ugly." Gavril was an atheist—a "convinced" non-believer. He felt himself go in a "body" that was "very dark and very cold." He traversed on a "road" made of "sharp stones." The devil was raising him from his bed. He saw "thousands" of demons and the devil told him there was a place prepared for him. Gavril was confused because though an atheist, he did not consider that he had done anything bad. He did not beat people. He was not cruel. And yet before him was eternal torment. For the first time in his life, he prayed. He begged God and promised, if rescued, to do His Will. Suddenly a white hand appeared between him and the devil, pointing at Gavril. He believes it was Jesus because the Voice could order the devil around. He told the devil that Gavril did not belong to him, placing Gavril with two angels. Joy flooded the Romanian. He was given a body of colorful light. He saw a "big gate." The angel told him "this is what it is like when everyone dies. The body decomposes in the grave but the spirit receives a body like this or like the demons." Remember, this is a man who was in the morgue for half a day. He was given a body as a "guest" in Heaven and told not to be afraid, that he needed to see a "piece" of eternity. "When I got to the gate, they pulled on me to go inside," he recounted. "I was afraid. How can I go there, in that beauty, that brightness . . . I am not worthy." But the angels told him not to be afraid and as he entered he felt as if he were walking on air. The joy was ineffable. He entered into what he said was "that big brightness, that big beauty" and like so many saw trees that seemed more than "a hundred meters" (three hundred feet) high. Every tree had all kinds of flowers. It was quite a contrast with the world of fire he saw—flames licking from the ground—before he saw Heaven. The Lord sends such people back to instruct us. There are deeper and deeper levels. It is said that upon death we are given that "robe" representing who we are. "The material had a thick weave to it, yet it had the softest feel of any material I had ever felt," a witness tells us. "It was softer than silk and it glowed. The color of the material was the whitest I have ever seen. The suit covered most of my body. Starting with a snug but comfortable neckline, it had full sleeves to my wrists, and full legs to my ankles. A curious part of the suit was that it had no openings such as those we need as humans." It is cottony. It reflects like glass that has been spun. Some see it, in Heaven, as materializing on them after they bathe in the "living waters." Others have seen heavenly entities making them at looms. In the nether regions, one is given a darkened body.

Compare Gavril with the account of Shawn Weed, a Marine from Louisiana who—like Gavril—first found himself in a dark place—perhaps we should say, two dark places.

Weed says he was out of his body and heading for that "other place" during an eight-minute death episode caused by a prank gone terrifyingly wrong. On a break from duty and horsing around ("chilling") with two Marine buddies (one a corporal, the other an S-2 intelligence agent), Weed put a noose around his neck for a macabre prank. They wanted to take a picture. They were toying with death, of course. Caught unsuspecting from behind by one of the men, who thought it would be even funnier to tighten the noose a bit, Weed, initially a willing participant in the prank, was immediately unable to inhale, unbeknown to his colleagues, who had snapped a few photographs of the "gag" and thought Weed was prolonging the stunt.

He was anything but. The Marine was unable to breathe. Desperate, he tried to loosen the noose. That proved impossible. Suddenly, he found himself there in the room, but in an entirely new way, now staring at his own body in the same room as his Marine buddies, who took an appallingly long while to notice that he was unconscious and in trouble. His spirit had left his body.

With equal suddenness, Weed next found himself *out* of the room and in a totally unfamiliar, otherworldly place, with darkness so thick and "solid black" it nearly had texture: a vast region that seemed to have no ground or floor, and yet with something that he was standing on, like air but hard, a place he didn't recognize at all: no light, no wind, no sound, as if in a giant warehouse, standing on nothing, motionless just like the place Gavril depicted. The only light was a dim one coming from his own form. He tried to stride forward and find an exit but felt stuck. "I had no clue where I was," he says. "I began to realize that I was standing in-between two parallel planes that stretch on forever and there's no walls, there's no doors, there's no windows, I'm trapped in between these two parallel planes, and there's no way out. From that point I became very scared but before I could even think of another thought I was snatched off of my feet by a very, very large demon. And of course for me, I didn't know what had happened. It was like getting hit by a truck and having no clue that it was ever coming. This thing had come upon me so fast and caught me with such complete surprise and was so big, I can't possibly begin to describe what it feels like to be in the grips of something that big. I had this shooting pain from my head to my feet, like a bolt of electricity but not stopping. And I had this pounding sensation, this hurting, pounding sensation from my left shoulder and I saw these fingers that came down to roughly to the bottom of my chest. The depth of its hands went from the side of my neck, the breadth of my shoulder. That was the width of its hand. The color of its skin was black and red. I don't know if it was red with black shadows moving across it or red with a black oily substance like a cloud moving beneath the skin so it makes it have a perception of moving while standing still, like the sky with clouds moving. I was watching these giant red fingers with blackness moving through them and this thing was crushing my left shoulder, had me and was just smiling at me, waiting for me to look at it. When I looked over my shoulder it was grotesque. It sounds even more crazy, but it was like thirteen feet tall. Anything you want to know in this place you can ask it in your mind and the answer is given to you and when I thought how big it was, 'thirteen feet' came to me. All I know is it was huge, ripped through with muscles. No hair, no beard. Just completely hairless and humanoid in shape—two legs, two arms, one mouth, one nose, two ears. The differences were this: where our eyes are white, its were yellow, and where our irises are green or blue or brown, its irises were gold and diamond-shaped like a snake's. It had a really wide flat nose and gleaming white teeth, perfectly shaped like a human's. The only thing strange about the teeth is where we have the canines, it had two tusks coming out of its mouth like a boar, a wild pig. The thing picked me up like I weighed nothing to it. And it was taking me along for a ride. I only looked at its face for a second. That's all it took. As a man, I'm not afraid of any other man on the face of this earth. I will fight any man, I don't care how much bigger they are than me. But this thing? There was no fighting it. It was far too big. It was like it weighed three or four thousand pounds. You could take one of me and put another on top of me and you still wouldn't be as tall. This thing had me by the shoulder and was moving at a very fast velocity. It felt like a hundred miles an hour and it had complete control. There was nothing, nothing at all, I could do to get away. I had seen that face for only a second and it was enough to scare me. I'm pretty sure it would scare anyone."

All hope drained from Weed. It seemed like it was all over.

"I think that the strength of hope is with God and without God and any hope you don't really have a reason to live and to fight and you don't have any strength whatsoever," he says in a video that has appeared on a number of internet sites. "Without hope you don't have strength. Hope left me, and it was taking me wherever it wanted to take me."

The thought came to him that they were headed from the "outer darkness" (what he later wondered is what the Bible calls "Abraham's bosom") toward a fiery part (the "fire and brimstone") of hell.

Like Gavril, this confused Weed. He was no saint. He was indifferent (or what the Bible says about being "lukewarm." Many nights he "drank like a fish" and smoked some cigarettes; slept around. Who knows what else? But he didn't consider himself a "bad" person. He was no murderer. He'd never molested a child. Occasionally he went to church. "I was just an average guy," he says, and so he found it "mortally appalling" that he was "being taken to hell."

"As I was thinking this to myself—that I'm not such a bad guy—that's when a pinprick of light appeared and I looked up at it—like a star far off in the night sky, something so tiny and insignificant and far away that it couldn't possibly help me. Then it moved off to the left a little bit and went back to the right. It moved and I wondered, 'What is that?' and I began focusing on it and it came rushing at me like—the only way I could describe it—the speed of this thing was like a bolt of lightning. It came at me so fast that one second it was just a tiny little star in the night sky and the next there was blinding white light and his hand was reaching down to me and it was an angel. [Here he begins to weep.]

"My hand just reached up and grabbed this hand, my reflex was just to grab this hand. And as soon as I touched this hand all three of us were motionless and standing on this ground that you can't see. This beast, this demon, still had me by the shoulder and instinctively I knew to stand still because I knew if I moved it would have ripped my shoulder and arm off and beaten me with it. It was just that massively strong. There was something in me telling me, 'Don't move. Don't move.'

"I was just standing there looking up at this angel and this angel was like nine feet six inches tall and had brown wavy hair pushed to the back and had olive-colored skin, it wasn't really white, it wasn't really black, it was somewhere in between, but the light that was emanating from within it was so bright white that it practically overshadowed the color of its skin. I say 'it' because it wasn't really a 'he' or a 'she,' although the body was shaped like a 'he,' like a male, and when you looked at its face it's like the most handsome man you have ever seen combined with the most beautiful woman you have ever seen. I mean, when you look at this angel, you think, 'Wow, he is beautiful.' I know this is a funny thing to say. In the vernacular, a man is 'handsome' and a woman is 'beautiful.' But this angel was just beautiful. Its eyes were blue—I mean *perfect* blue. If someone took a piece of the sky and put it in its eyes, or a cup from the ocean, and put it in its eyes, there were no flaws in them. Just perfect. Just beautiful. He was shaped like a man with a chest and strong arms and an Adam's apple, a strong man, more like fitness-trainer strong, not body-builder strong, like the demon, with muscles popping from where they shouldn't be, but you can tell this angel was there to fight and he had on a white robe cut in a v-neck in the front and gold along the edge of his collar like embroidered and this robe was kind of like a white Roman tunic than came just before below his knees and elbows and I was just blown away by it. I'm looking up at it and blown away by its brightness and beauty and at the same time frozen in place and you could feel [the] anger [from the demon] like heat and it looked around to see what had stopped it: It turned around and was ready to fight, make no mistake; this demon was ready to get down in the worst way—but as it whipped around, this angel—its speed was just incredible and it just rushed forward and with open palm hit this demon and had to angle its arm upwards at about the height of its head to hit this demon in the chest and it hit this demon with such power—I can't describe the fierceness of it, the power of this thing. It hit this demon with such force that its hand was literally ripped from my shoulder and it had no clue what had hit him. By the time it turned its head it was already hit. And this demon was hit with such force that it literally folded up and flew backwards."

The angel—according to this Marine—then called Weed by a "long" mystical moniker.

"It called me this name to let me know more or less that I still had a chance to make it into Heaven, that I had a heavenly name, and that I squandered it, I wasted it, and if this had been my ultimate time, that's where I would have stayed. When he called me this long name, it was a feeling of 'home.'"

The name was just as quickly removed from his memory.

"It looked at me and it began to speak at me and its voice was like a waterfall. If a waterfall could speak, like a rushing sound *(S-s-shawn)*, I understood it was converting my understanding to understanding its language. It didn't descend down to my broken language of English. It elevated me up to understand its language and he looked at me and said, *'Hello, my name is Michael.'* [Weed weeps again.] I immediately knew this was the Archangel of the Bible."

The demon was trying to return, claims Weed, and the angel "gave me a saddened look and he said, *'You're time has not yet come. It's time for you to go.'*" Immediately the Marine was back in his body, as immediately as he had left. He opened his eyes and was back in the room with his friends, lying on the sofa they had placed him on. It took twenty minutes to recover use of his body, as they tried to revive him (successfully, happily, for all three Marines).

These are people who are shown parts of eternity and allowed to return so as to instruct us.

Weed's message was to devote life to God as much as you possibly can. It's not enough to say you believe. You must believe. It's not enough to not be a killer, or an abuser. You must be holy. "If that makes a Bible-thumping Christian, so be it," says the Marine. "I'd rather be a Bible-thumping Christian than in the 'middle,' because I know where that gets you (*Revelation* 3:20). We don't realize the reality of the place. I was at the doorstep of hell. I know for certain that it does exist because that's where [before Michael] it was taking me."

Chapter 4

When we have darkness in us, we may have demons around us—attached to us.

These entities can attack at death.

Shedding them now, on earth, is a good idea.

Donning the whitest robe we can makes sense.

Every day, and every minute, we have a priceless opportunity to purge what we don't want to take into the afterlife, what we don't want to "pack."

For this is the term that must be used: afterlife, not just Heaven. There are levels of Heaven and hell and then there is purgatory and levels in this great "laundromat" in the sky—countless ones, at least by earthly calculation. One level turns into another, and the partition between earth and Heaven and perhaps between Heaven and purgatory is like a glass door folding back on itself. I actually hear such renditions. After death, we are totally revealed; we have no shame; we're like Adam and Eve in the Garden (before the fall). But here, in Heaven, the garden is protected against Satan. Unless the soul has descended to hell, the devil can no longer touch us. His demons have no sway. They can't enter. They can't even enter the deepest part of purgatory (where there may be fire similar to Gehenna). There is also no more failure. There is no more ego. Once in His embrace, there is no more evil. There is no money. You possess only who and what you are and what you know and how you serve God. You will (eventually) see all He has created and feel so loved it will be like you are the only one in existence—His sole child.

This is a little attempt at conveying the ineffable.

The point is that joy awaits us and can be reached immediately. That's right: upon death, we can get right to glory if we don't take what we are not supposed to take with us!

Otherwise, we settle to the level of the hereafter (in most cases, purgatory) where we belong, where we must be purged not just of sin, but of imperfections, where, due to the state of our souls, we are most comfortable.

A perfect place requires perfect cleanliness.

It sounds impossible, but it's within your reach.

The key is to treat every moment as if it is your last. You have to plan. You have to want to get to the highest heights without going through the lowest depths (the bottom, as it were, of the valley).

If you were going on a long journey, would you want to be carrying much? Would you set out for a walk across the country dragging large bags?

What happens when you take things in excess?

It costs more at the airport. It bogs you down on the way to the taxi. It clutters your hotel room. You have more to dig through. You lose things. Important items can be obscured. This is all because you are bringing unnecessary items that are more about your imperfections than your clarity. (Makes it tougher to be screened through airport security, which is similar to a narrow gate, doesn't it?)

If you're going on a trip, would you bring worn socks? Would you bring dirty clothes? Would you take pants or a jacket with holes in them? Would the coat you decide to take be threadbare?

Going through security, would you try to hide something?

These are metaphors for the spiritual transition into Heaven. We bring only who we are and the love we have and the good works and the nice thoughts. We go only with faith. The rest must be left behind. *Nothing that reflects negatively on your spirit will be allowed through the final entry into paradise.*

In the afterlife, your life will flash before you in intricate detail and will not be just a viewing, like a movie, or hologram (though it will have some of those qualities), but a *reliving.* There is no time in the realm of God and so it is nothing for Him to reverse time and replay and hover upon every moment of particular relevance.

A key is to view everything we do as if we are on a stage, in front of a camera, as if we will see it again—because we will!

Make a list of what you *don't* want to take.
You don't want to take resentment.
You don't want to take dislike.
You don't want to take jealousy.
You don't want to take grief.
You don't want to take depression.
You don't want to take over-attachment.
You don't want any obsession.
You don't want lust.
You don't want to take sin of any kind.
You don't want to take thoughts that are vengeful.
You don't want to take thoughts that are spiteful.
You don't want to take *anything* you have not forgiven.
You don't want to take trauma.

You don't want to take the occult.

You don't want to take self-righteousness.

You don't want to take anger.

You don't want to take irritation.

You don't want to take pride.

You don't want to take anything that is a *physical* possession (a clear sign you aren't ready for the eternal).

You don't want to take sloth.

You don't want to take a lie—not one.

You don't want to bring umbrage.

You don't want to take anxiety.

You don't want to take judgmentalism.

You do not want to be burdened with fear.

You don't want to bring bias.

You don't want to bring slander, gossip.

You don't want to bring self-centeredness.

You don't want to bring selfishness.

You don't want to bring an addiction.

You don't want to bear gluttony.

You would not want to carry any of the cardinal transgressions.

You do not want to bring avarice, boastfulness, or contempt.

You do not want to bring nastiness.

You do not want to bring high-handedness.

You don't want to bring vanity—not an ounce, not even in your "carry-on."

Hatred would be the number one thing to discard—hatred and pride.

You don't want to bring guilt, or materialism.

The list is long and goes on and you can formulate your own.

In prayer, the Holy Spirit will guide you.

When you haven't left such things behind, when they have not yet been cast out, they're an albatross. They are chains. They weigh you down and attach you to people or things. There is a "soul-tie." It's like *A Christmas Carol.* Many don't realize this: when we haven't forgiven a person, or bear jealousy, we're bound spiritually to that person until what binds us is released. "The souls of men and women can knit together with negative repercussions," a deliverance minister once explained. "A domineering mother's soul knitted to her son's, and he ended up in an insane asylum suffering from schizophrenia. When the woman cut the spiritual umbilical cord and cast it off, the son recovered instantly and several days later left the asylum, normal. Manipulation and control by another person may create negative soul ties."

He added: "Often the souls of ex-lovers knit together, even though they may no longer see each other. They may marry others, but they continue to be tormented by thoughts of the former lover. Strange circumstances may bring them together, and they bump into each other at unlikely times and places. Even if their relationship ended on a sour note, they often think of, fantasize about, and lust for each other. Their soul ties need to be broken and cast off."

So must any form of darkness.

I once knew a former New York City transit officer (later a volunteer fireman) named John P. McNamara who was at a fireman's parade in Peekskill and afterward attended a party where he drank too much in a forty-foot tower outside of town where I presume they did training. "Except for the section where the metal stairs were, the room was enclosed by a walkway with a three-foot-high metal railing going around the other three sides," he recalled. "A person could look right through the metal openings to the concrete sidewalk below.

"I walked out of the room to get some fresh air. The sun was directly below my eyes and before I knew it I hit the rail with my body—waist-high—and went over.

"*Then it happened.* In the blink of an eye, I saw forty feet of concrete coming up to meet me. I saw every scene of my life flash before my eyes. The only words I could say were, 'God help me!' Just then a hand yanked my right arm back to the top of the handrail. I pulled myself back over and stood there clutching the rail with both hands and shaking like a leaf. When I turned around I stood looking at someone who looked like me, except his uniform was immaculate! I said, 'Thanks. You saved my life!' He smiled and said, *'It's not your time, John.'* Then he walked over to the steps and started going down. I lost sight of him for a second. When I got to the steps, he was gone."

Chapter 5

An angel? Almost assuredly. But with a message.

He was showing John with his neat attire and a clean-shaven, sober face how he was supposed to look; what he was supposed to fix in his life; how he was supposed to change, if he wanted his life back. He was leading John to shed baggage and fulfill the design God had for him. What John was shown was how to look if one wants to meld with the Kingdom of Heaven. The angel was presenting the person John was meant to be—clean, smiling, compassionate.

Would an angel look drunken? Would an angel be unkempt? Would an angel have a sullied aura? Would an angel look unmanicured? Would an angel stumble around?

When you die, you want to be a pure soul.

This means shedding what prevents you from being as clear and pure as when you entered life as an infant.

That takes discipline.

Discipline is a critical key, perhaps *the* critical key, to purification.

Discipline is prayer. Discipline is restraint. Discipline is diligence.

A test of life is facing all the temptations, pitfalls, and sludge yet somehow clearing it all away before the passage, wiping everything from the blackboard—getting back to *initial innocence.* It's why (*Matthew* 18:3) Jesus said, *"Truly, I say to you, unless you turn and become like children, you will never enter the kingdom of Heaven."*

You must clear the slate. We all can. We consider it an insult to be called "infantile" or a "baby."

It's the way God Himself came to this earth: with humble simplicity.

The Infant.

This concept is as incredible as it is life-changing: that a key spiritual chore during this journey on earth is simply to get back to how we were, as far as purity, when we entered.

In many ways, the birth into this world mimics the exit.

A newborn goes through a tunnel. So will we, on the way out. A baby arrives from the darkness of a womb into the sudden blinding brilliance of delivery-room lights. We will enter an even more brilliant (but not blinding) Light. A baby makes its requests loudly, directly, and simply. So also must we pray from the heart. An infant has total trust in its parents. We must have total trust in Christ. A newborn wears nothing and yet bears no shame. Once purged, we'll feel likewise, swathed in white. A newborn loves unconditionally; to this must we likewise aspire. An infant pleads with no guile, no ulterior motive, no deception.

A newborn is simple.

A baby is accepting.

A child lives a life knowing that what he or she needs will be fulfilled, as we must also have faith.

Children find joy in every little thing.

So should we.

Joy brings us to direct entry into Heaven!

I saw an interview with a woman who came back from a close call with death and couldn't believe she had never appreciated the incredible beauty—the simple, everyday colors—of the world God has created around us.

What surrounds us will reflect what is inside of us. It will mirror us.

Do you want to look at the world through a glass darkly?

Do you want to die feeling miserable?

It does happen: there are those who die into their darkness.

A doctor named Reggie Anderson who logs deathbed experiences tells of a man named Eddie who was dying of cancer and had a terrible temper, even a history of drunken knife fights (a man who, says Dr. Anderson, "treated his children horribly and didn't care whether they lived or died," abused them, and wanted to hear nothing about Jesus). "I listened to him as he struggled to take each breath," testified the physician. "Unlike many of the believers I'd witnessed who had crossed silently and peacefully, Eddie seemed to be struggling. He made grunting noises and clung to each breath as if it were his last. Eventually his breathing slowed, and the grunts became less frequent. When his last breath finally came, it wasn't the same peaceful exhale that I'd become so familiar with in my other dying patients. Eddie fought to take a final breath, and then his pulse and heart stopped. His last breath was a grunt.

"Suddenly, I felt some type of dark cloud present in the room.

"The lights grew dimmer, and the temperature plummeted. The room was freezing cold as though the temperature had instantly dropped a hundred degrees. The warmth I'd come to expect when Heaven's door opened seemed to have been replaced by the opening of a liquid nitrogen canister.

"The room appeared dark and shadowy, as if it were being swallowed by a black abyss.

"That's when I smelled sulfur and diesel. The air felt heavy, and it got harder to breathe. I remembered the same smell from a [place] after a [case of murders]. Memories of those dark days flooded my mind. I was terrified. Though I had no rational reason to feel this way, I was afraid I would get trapped and be unable to leave. I wanted to get out as fast as I could."

Dr. Anderson hurried down the hall and turned on the hot water in a sink, desperate to cleanse himself. "Evil had entered the room," he recounted. "I quickly made the death pronouncement and left. I wanted to wash the darkness off me."

What was *in* Eddie had now materialized on the outside; it was now a force, an accompaniment—and a destination. Obviously, most of you are not where Eddie was. But there *is* darkness. I watched the video of a man named Bryan Melvin who was also a non-believer and succumbed to cholera from water brought back by a friend who had visited Mexico. During his brush with death Melvin arrived in a "very dark black void" through a tunnel that went round and round, roaring and roaring, "spinning and spinning and spinning," to a place he called "the pit" where there were loud noises, screeches, screams, and a strange slurping, with horrible smells like sulfur and intense heat and beings who resembled deceased people, including some he knew, but in reality were demons: what looked like his best friend turning into "something unreal"; some with eyes that were reptile-like, "filthy smelly" creatures that "started to come at me" and grab at him and a huge reptilian entity that spat at the terrified construction worker and spoke a language he could barely understand—indicating to come forward, where Melvin saw the end of a horizon and vast mountains that the creature "ripped open" like a veil. The next thing Melvin knew he was on a dusty road peering into "cubes" or cells: compartments piled side by side and on top of each other like crates in endless rows, some vacant, some with people embedded in the very walls, reliving parts of their pasts: nightmares without end. "I followed the rank creature and immediately emerged on the other side of the horizon," he wrote. "A wide, dirty, flat, barren expanse of land gently sloped downward, betraying an endless circular spiral of misery. On the left side of the coiled grade were rows and rows of cubes with more cubes columned high, forming a wall of ten-by-ten-foot partitions mirroring the events displayed inside. Each cube was stacked six high. You could see into these but not out of them. Within every chamber resided an individual person, trapped, unable to escape . . . Turning, I saw the lizard-like entity a few feet from me, reaching its ugly, greenish-yellow arms as if to drag me away to a desperate fate . . ." What he saw, he said, can best be described in *Ezekiel* 32:22-23 ("All of them are slain, fallen by the sword, whose graves are set in the remotest parts of the pit and her company is round about her grave. All of them are slain, fallen by the sword, who spread terror in the land of the living").

This was only a small part of hell, which he realized is an "enormous place."

Over and again, the demon would tear off Melvin's arm and shoulder, beat him with it, and then his shoulder and arm would grow back and be torn off again. The same was true of those in the "cubes": they were to be dismembered or mutilated in some other fashion only to be "healed" and dismembered again.

He saw a temple prostitute who'd sacrificed babies to pagan statues for payment and had died in 69 A.D. and was still being tortured by demons in the guise of those infants. He also saw a woman who practiced witchcraft in olden times and now was trapped in a coffin. Similarly, a lady who had danced around fire in homage to the nature gods was in a cell where she was smacked unrelentingly with stones (she thought the earth, not God, was her savior). He also claimed to have seen a man he identified as Hitler in a cube and burning in flames with a hideous look on his face, all the tortures coming back to him, reduced to ashes and then made whole so he could be burned again, suffering every single thing he had inflicted on others.

(Melvin was saved when—like Weed, and Barnut, and so many others, whose testimonies are remarkably consistent—he cried out to the Lord.)

Jesus, Jesus, Jesus.

The person you take to Heaven—or hell, or purgatory—as the real "you" will be surrounded by spirits that are *similar* to you. They will be familiar.

You don't want to take (or meet up with) a demon.

I viewed the video of a man who nearly drowned. While they tried to revive him, he found himself heading to a dark place where there were two little fires, like torches.

Despite misgivings, he headed toward these flames. Soon he saw a heap of gold—coins, goblets, perhaps also jewelry—and sitting atop of this pile was the devil or a major demon, with a bull's head and curved horns but a human face. Had this—wealth—been his preoccupation?

Assailed when he "died," an atheist named Dr. Howard Storm said "demons" who attacked him, hurling unspeakable curses at him, and leading him to hell, reflected his own state of being.

"They started to push and pull at me," he told a television interviewer. "Because of their own emptiness, and their own torment, the only way they could relate was to bring someone else to their same place. They wanted me to be part of them. *The horrible part of this is that I was one of them.* I know that in many respects they were my kindred brothers and sisters—and I was not a stranger to them, or them to me. All they were doing was initiating me into their world of loneliness, hopelessness, and despair, ultimately meaning their lack of God, their lack of love. The Bible says love is God and God is love. These were people who had rejected all of that, and when they left this world, they were living what they basically saw all their lives."

Loneliness, hopelessness, and despair—rejection of God—were now not just their inner thinking but their environment.

That's one way we create a negative hereafter.

Emotions carry over into eternity. There are many mansions.

There are also, as Melvin saw, many dungeons.

Are you condemning yourself? Is a negative self-image causing you to descend into deeper darkness?

"Our thoughts have exceptional power to draw on the negative or positive energies around us," says the most famous of afterlife chronicles. "When they draw at length on the negative, the result can be a weakening of the body's defenses. This is especially true when our negative thoughts are centered on ourselves. I understood that we are at our *most* self-centered state when we are depressed. Nothing can sap our spiritual strength and health as much as prolonged depression. But when we make the effort to move ourselves away from self and begin to concentrate on the needs of others and how to serve them, we begin to heal. Service is a balm to both the spirit and the body."

We know we are advancing in the right way when we can summon joy even on those "disastrous" days (knowing that God is above any calamity). Life is a test. There are good days and bad days. A great day is followed by a less-than-great one.

As a researcher named Kenneth Ring noted, "Joy in living is the truest sign that we are living right. What kills is judgment; what heals is love.

"The Light itself is only love and it never judges; instead, it gently *nudges* you toward your essential self. When you become identified with this Light, you will have only love and compassion for yourself—and for everything—and you will be able to let go of all judgment."

There is always the caution that the "light" can be a deception. We have to be careful if an account does not include Jesus Christ of Nazareth. The devil can come as an "angel of light." Take what is good and leave the rest. Beware the New Age.

But we also know that God is Light—it's how He struck down Saint Paul!—and that He's also Love.

Love heals. Love cleanses.

Through life, we pick up grit.

It's our chore to get rid of that.

Let's return to infants.

A baby is authentic. A baby is totally honest. A baby is his or her essential, pure self. A baby has faith that all its needs will be addressed. A baby cries out—from the heart—when those needs are not met. A baby has no guilt.

This is worth a moment of your consideration: Looking at your life, right now, what are you guilty about? What still needs to be repaired? What steals your joy (and peace of mind)? What do you need to make right? What's unsettled in your conscience?

As one man, a doctor named George Ritchie who had been an atheist, but had the death revelation, said: guilt is the darkest, deepest, and most potent emotion, and it can take eons to peel off the layers separating souls in bondage to it. "I saw people in this state and felt their immeasurable loneliness, fear, and utter coldness," said this man, who became a psychiatrist, alluding to souls imprisoned *by their own* emotions. On the other hand, there is the story of a man with his family in a horrible concentration camp who chose to make the experience a joyful one for his young boy—such that the boy's memories of it were not unpleasant!

This is victory.

It is freedom, no matter what.

Allow nothing to imprison you.

Anything is possible.

Ask: What emotions hold you back? What failures continue to repeat? Does anything imprison you?

Where have you *not* sought self-forgiveness (as well as God's)? Have you repeated and then made the real effort to change?

We are what we repeat.

If it's a negative, when you repeat yourself, you defeat yourself.

Chapter 6

Birds of a feather flock together.

If we can't forgive (including ourselves), the souls around us may be equally unforgiving.

I need to emphasize this point: self-condemnation.

Before we forgive others—which is so very paramount (in forming a bright hereafter)—we must forgive ourselves: go through your life and exonerate yourself for sin, stupidity, wrong-thinking, misjudgment, presumption, and ignorance, as you also seek forgiveness from God through Confession (which breaks initial bonds, opening the door to expiation).

"Work with love and kindness in all you do, every second of every day," said Dr. Ritchie, summarizing the lessons he learned. "Forgive yourself when you fail."

"Take this rule, whenever you fall into a fault, be it great or small, even though you may have committed the same four thousand times in a day, and always voluntarily and with advertency: never allow yourself to fall into a state of morose bitterness, and do not be disquieted, nor waste your time by scrutinizing yourself. But at once acknowledge what you have done, and, humbly regarding your own weakness, turn lovingly to your God, and say to Him with your lips, or with your mind only, 'Lord, I have done this, being what I am, and nothing else could be expected from me, save only these and similar faults, and I would not have stopped where I did, had not Thy goodness lifted me up and continued with me. I give Thee thanks for that from which Thou hast preserved me, and I grieve over that which I have done through not corresponding with Thy grace. Pardon me, and give me grace that I may never offend Thee anymore, and may nothing ever separate me from Thee, whom I desire ever to serve and to obey.' Having done this, do not waste time in anxious thoughts, imagining that the Lord has not forgiven you. But, in a spirit of faith and repose, continue your exercises, as if you had not fallen at all," wrote Lorenzo Scuploi in his classic *The Spiritual Combat.*

Confession "saves" the soul.

Expiation cleanses it.

Heaven is unity and harmony as the music ascends.

Find harmony—first with yourself.

That harmony will bring health.

It will also bring a beauty that flows into the frequencies of the eternal.

A higher frequency is a better place.

Don't remain in a dark place.

Move on from sorrow, lest you attract more darkness.

It is all in your attitude.

Misery piles on misery.

You keep attracting it.

In Heaven, everything breathes love in and out. There, we are complete and whole.

When you're obstinate, when you stiffen your neck, when you're lackadaisical, when you pooh-pooh the little things, when you simply don't want to address something (whether through laziness or pride, which is stubbornness, or simply through ignorance, due to a lack of prayer), when you are divisive, you are not ready for the higher realms. Your spirit resonates in a way that is sluggish.

Often, the little resistances in life are hints.

God warns. He sends signs.

Heed them.

There are no coincidences. When things occur, we must ask the Holy Spirit to discern them. We don't need other people to "read the signs" (except perhaps for a spiritual director). God speaks most "loudly" about your life to you—not intermediaries. Truth recognized (and applied to your life) is wisdom.

It's hard but: confess failings, ask forgiveness, forgive yourself, and move on: forget your shortcomings, once you have corrected them.

In time, God will remove the residue (or "debt") from transgressions.

Those who repent and accept the sacrifice of Jesus will be redeemed by God and thus not be judged as guilty before Him (says *1 Thessalonians* 4:13–18). When those who die glimpse hell, and are rescued by hands, often those Hands have wounds in them (this was the case with Barnut and Melvin). We are raised with His Blood. Believe that and just stop repeating your failures. Break the cycle by simply doing what is right and forcing yourself to halt what's wrong—just stop it. You have the willpower. If it's negative, critical thoughts about every person who pops into your head, train yourself (in prayer) to immediately see everyone as eighty percent or more good, instead of focusing on the smaller proportion that bears faults.

At first it can be like a cyclone: halting in the midst of it may cause it to sweep first one way, then another against you, but eventually the "eye" of the storm (raised by the devil) will pass, debris will settle, and the storm will clear. "He has sent me to proclaim freedom for the prisoners and recovery of sight for the blind, to set the oppressed free," says *Luke* 4:18.

We often fashion our own captivity and take that captivity into eternity when we die under a burden of guilt, regret, or shame, as well as sin that is not expiated. This confines us to the "tunnel" or even makes us fear the Light. *When we judge ourselves too harshly*, we're assuming the role of God while forgetting His Mercy.

No one who has had a near-death experience has ever described Him as anything other than the most loving Person they have ever encountered.

God is light. Mercy is light. Life comes from light. Life comes from His Light. Light is love and since God is love we see how it all dovetails into a simple equation: love equals Heaven and Heaven equals ultimate freedom. In Heaven, the freedom is such that you don't even really walk there. There are no physical constraints. You move as if gliding above the "ground." You can think and suddenly be somewhere distant. We don't leave the ground, however, when we bring the "chains" of earth with us. Never forget the crucial fact that God loves us. No matter what you've done, He loves you. He loves every single person on earth, equally. Said a woman named Nancy Clark during an interview with a researcher, "Before my experience, I guess I was like most people struggling with a better self-image. But I really *experienced* how precious and how loved I am by God and I am constantly reminded of that in my daily life. I often think, 'If He values me so much, then no matter what bad thoughts I may think about myself, I *have* to be a worthwhile person.'" Added a woman named Peggy: "I was shown how much all people are loved. It was overwhelmingly evident that the Light loved everyone equally without any conditions. I really want to stress this because it made me so happy to know we didn't have to believe or do certain things to be loved. We already were and are, no matter what. If people could only know how much they're loved, maybe they wouldn't feel so scared anymore."

Remember that with all your faults (and we all have them), God still chose to give you life. He chose to give you a mission.

Self-accusation can come from the Great Accuser (the devil) who wants you weighed down in guilt.

You are no good. God finds you repulsive. You will never be forgiven. Do you see why we must balance introspection (a healthy look at ourselves) with self-forgiveness?

God chose to love you. He chose to give you a *unique identity.*

You have unique friends.

They will not be lost to you.

You don't want to bring bad memories.

You don't want to bring shame.

You don't want to bring guilt.

You don't want them as part of your landscape.

Expiate—atone for your sins—and go forward.

You're part of His Plan.

Have compassion for yourself—"self-love"—but not the wrong *kind* of self-love.

That wrong kind is puffed-up, self-centered, and selfish, which obscures—and even disfigures—your essence.

Purely, like a child, you must *want* to want God.

Here we tap into His Love.

And boy is it there!

"If you took the love of my grandmother and multiplied it by a million times, maybe you could get the intensity of this love I felt from God," testified a former atheist and near-deather named Barbara. "A baby in a crib became the center of a cloud of bubbles and in each bubble was a scene from my life. I bounced through all these bubbles and re-experienced my life and everything including what the other people in the bubble experienced too. I wasn't just re-experiencing it myself, but with my mother and my dad and my brother and my boyfriend who became my husband and then my kids—I was them as well as me—and I could feel the love and I could also feel the negative."

In Heaven we no longer bear grudges, no longer feel negativity, no longer resent anything or anyone; the bitterness, the differences we had on earth, evaporate after purgation. We are all connected. We will see that. When one of us fails, we all do. Thus, we should never want someone else to fall. We are connected to everyone and everything. "There was such joy that I could feel him again," related a woman who encountered her deceased father, with whom she had been at odds just before his death. "I said, 'There must have been times when you were disappointed in me, that you were angry with me, for the things that I thought, for the things I was doing.' He said, 'Here, nothing is judged. The [hurts] that happened in life have no meaning here.'"

Guilt, insults, and grudges are left at the door of Heaven.

So is worry.

There is no place for that in Heaven.

You never die there. No one is out to do you harm. There is no disease. You can't go broke. You don't need money.

Fear is among the very most negative of all emotions. It's something that Satan inspires. He does this to siphon energy from you.

Instead, what we take to Heaven should be knowledge, love, and memories.

In the eternal is a realm in which all knowledge awaits us in a timeless state: no past, no present, no future. Those states will all coexist as one "now." It is spatial—not linear. Here is where there will be illumination and enlightenment. You will seem to have complete knowledge. It is inexpressible. You will never understand it in human terms. All questions will be answered as soon as they are thought. It may be just after the life review. Accessible there will be secrets of the ages—from the very beginning, proceeding without end. The mysteries of the universe will be resolved. As the Bible promises, all things will be revealed. On earth we spend a great deal of time fashioning masks but these masks will be removed. In that sense, there will be a sense of exposure. Some say even gender is taken away, though others say it remains. Love and knowledge stand most prominently in what we keep. Not one of your thoughts is lost. Your identity is secure, just seen differently. God doesn't want you to carry guilt, says a man who was "there." You must understand that He forgives you anything if it is requested from the heart. "When you make a mistake you need to consider what you did and why you did it," an angel told this fellow. "You should seek a better alternative. Tell God in the clearest way you know what you did, why you did it, and what you are going to do about it. Before you can ask God's forgiveness you will receive God's forgiveness. God will erase your mistake from the Collective Memory of your life if, and only if, you are genuinely ready to be forgiven. You must regret your mistake and try to never repeat it again. God wants you to succeed." He wants you to be filled with joy. We exist in this world for one purpose—to love God—and we accomplish that by doing His Will through love of others. "Anything else is immaterial," the angel stated. You must accept His forgiveness. He is insulted when you do not, and you may remain in a "nether" zone. The same happens with fear.

Fear is a lack of faith—or better put, negative faith: we have faith that a negative will occur. It is faith in a negative. This gives the negative a better chance of occurring. *Fear of the devil is faith in the devil.* Just as faith in God puts us more in touch with His Power, fear is faith in evil and adds to its ability to affect us (and those around us).

"If on earth we had loved Him as we ought to have done, there would not be so many of us here in this place of expiation," said a nun who was in purgatory (and appearing to a living nun).

Inertia and idleness draw darkness. They bring the enemy, who bears chains. Life was not designed to waste. Every minute counts. The Lord is perfect. We must seek perfection every minute but without self-condemnation (except when it is warranted).

With the Lord on our lips—*"Jesus, I trust in You; Jesus I trust in You"*—and with Mary in our thoughts in difficult moments—*"Mary take over; Mary take over"*—we have the area code and phone number to Heaven. Along with peace, joy forms the state of "well-being" that melds with Heaven.

Chapter 7

Like a child, be joyful. This will lead you to your "mission." There's a tree in Heaven, according to Barnut, that represents your deeds. "When I entered there, I saw two beds and a table with a bowl and a small tree in it," he testified. "That tree was approximately thirty to forty centimeters [about a foot] in height. The angel told me, *'This is how much your good deeds developed here.'*"

Let your tree tower.

Deeds come from your mission and your mission in life, the blueprint since you were "knitted" in the womb (*Psalm* 139:13), can be in what you love doing, what you have energy for, what comes naturally, what gives you a sense of contentment, what makes you happy, what fits your personality, what's done without selfishness, what coincides with how you were made mentally and physically but more than anything spiritually.

Simply put, your mission fits like an old shoe.

Those you are close to hint at your mission.

Your spouse is there to help you learn love.

"Our assignment is programmed in at birth and it is the very thing or things we love most," intoned that woman named Peggy. "I always thought doing what you loved most was selfish. I can remember how amazed and happy I was when [the above] information came to my mind!"

Every person has a mission that's a cog in the fulfillment of what God has created.

Instead of time, there is a perpetual unfolding of "now."

Pursue the contentment of your heart.

When we stray from our assignments, trouble may ensue; there may be a "series of unfortunate events." We're unfulfilled. We are discontent. We want others to make us happy. When you're doing what you were meant (and *made*) to do (what is in your spiritual "DNA"), a bliss comes that opens a "door" of light. Grace pours forth.

"As this stream of pure love went through me, I felt as if the light was saying simultaneously, 'I love you *completely* and *entirely* as you are, *because you are.*"

In His Light, you will appear far more handsome or beautiful than you can imagine. I noticed this around the mystic Maria Esperanza: when you took a photograph with her, you always looked better. She emanated God's Light—and He sees the best in us and reflects the best back. We must learn to reflect back the best in others. Once in Heaven, there is no harsh light. There will be no imperfection. Your heart generates splendiferous hues. "The colors made me say, 'Oh, how good it is here, I never want to leave!'" said Barnut.

They switch back and forth, the colors, like a chimera without end in this place where things are formed of light: solid and yet not solid, opaque on one side, transparent on the other.

"The colors would flow with the music, each wave of scintillating 'fire-color' weaving through the sounds as they emanated from the center, like an explosion of choreographed fireworks accompanying the music," said a man who died at age fifteen and wished to remain anonymous. "The sounds were the colors . . . and the colors were the source of the sound: pure harmony rising from one stanza to the next and reaching a crescendo only to fade out into the next phase, ever-building to a climax but never reaching it; music without beat, without end, timeless, eternal, pure.

"I was stunned. Nothing on earth was anything like this music of color blended with sound; had I a body, I would have exploded in sheer joy at just five seconds of exposure to this eternal symphony."

It will accompany the music of your soul which is the goodness of you resonating with your name.

"Vast jungles," went on this fellow. "Parks . . . majestic mighty mountains . . . oceans the size of earth itself . . . and lakes as big as oceans. Waterfalls a hundred kilometers high . . . mighty rivers packed with life . . . crystal-clear . . . the trees . . . small and great . . . colorful . . . detailed . . . each one unique and some full of flowers of colors vivid and bright . . . some full of fruit of weird shapes and hue. All was alive . . . not just living things . . . but living beings . . . not just alive . . . they were in its essence . . . each leaf . . . blade of grass . . . creature and fish . . . bird and reptile . . . were not just alive: it's like they were emanating life. This mighty and majestic landscape went on and on.

"What I thought were small hills in the distance turned out to be mighty mountain ranges that make the Himalayas look like a badly thought up joke in comparison. The waterfall immediately to my left upon arrival there, wow, it was over three hundred kilometers [nearly two hundred miles] from where I floated and even at that distance so utterly magnificent . . . rising up and up, above eye level, like looking up at a river. It descended down the side of a 'small' (compared to some of the other mountains there) hundred-kilometer-high [sixty-mile-high] cliff face . . . falling . . . cascading . . . majestic . . . and throwing off rainbows in its mighty mist . . . I saw benches, tables, set along the river under the trees. People and beings alike would sit and talk, smiling, laughing, some in deep thought or conversation, some being serious, some being light-hearted, like they were contemplating some new revelation they had just stumbled upon.

"In all it was a very busy yet relaxed scene. The trees themselves were amazing. Mighty branches spread out in majestic awnings of life over the river and the benches below. I saw fruit in the trees: gold, green, orange, purple, blue, all sorts of colors. People were picking the fruit and casually eating it; there were no scraps, no pips or skins left over."

The homes?

"Take your basic hovel there for example . . . the lowest of the simple buildings," he said. "I focused upon one just to burn into my memory what the least of the creative powers the Master Builder is capable of. It was about the size of your average house here on earth but was constructed of pure elements. There were no bricks or mortar, no alloys or mixtures. Each part of that building was pure element: the windows, framed with a rich ebony-like substance, shot through with gold veins, each pane looking like pure diamond or crystal. The walls of the house were like a sort of moonstone, opaque and solid yet light flowed in and through the walls themselves like a fiber-optic cable in actual application, the light taken from all around and magnifying throughout the house. The windows would break the light into amazing colors and decorate the interior with rainbows of fantastic hue, then the walls would absorb and magnify the light and send it streaming outward to the house next to it. The process would repeat along each house—all sharing this amazing visual display and amplifying it to its peak, only to send it along again to the next dwelling, and the next.

"I was utterly flabbergasted. What a design, and the Mind Who thought up this amazing idea of optical brilliance must be unfathomable!"

He is certainly that and has designed this place for souls who have been purged, have let go of what they had to let go. They have brought only what they should. It is important to bring *desire*. We must desire to be in a high place near God. There are places in Heaven for everyone on earth, we are told, but some go empty. Incredibly, those for whom they were constructed have rejected them. Everything is filled with joy and worship and tone. Those who do not want that as a surrounding go elsewhere. Your mansion is your mission. We purify on earth so that we belong in the place that has been prepared—we purify and grow. It is important to grow, but never to assess how someone else is doing. You can't know! Their lives were designed to accomplish certain (often hidden) things. Talents grow when used for God. When your gifts enlarge, you are fulfilling your purpose. If your work allows you to love fully, it is part of your mission.

When we're honest about what's wrong we open ourselves to release it. A breeze blows through. We leave behind residue, taking only our highest attributes. Sin becomes ash. The ash is taken windward. This is expiation, which often involves suffering because when we suffer we part from the flesh. We rise above it. We elevate. We burn off imperfection. Our blinders drop. We can see more from a cross. We begin to perceive with the eyes of eternity. Suddenly we have an entirely different perspective. Traumas or disease or other major events—especially when sudden and radical, when they're debilitating—cause a curtain to part just as the veil of the Temple was rent upon the Crucifixion of Jesus (*Matthew* 57:17).

Chapter 8

A "jolt" is often required. There is the famous account of the dentist from Bogota, Colombia, named Dr. Gloria Polo I alluded to, who met death after she was struck by lightning on May 5, 1995. At first, upon rising from her horribly scarred body, she was allowed to glimpse Heaven. But soon after, she saw purgatory and hell and went through her "judgment": shown how arrogant she had been, how attached to money, how lustful, how critical, how obsessed with her physique, how mesmerized by astrology, how errant in having an abortion and even funding the abortions of younger women.

"I saw the reality of my life, and felt much sadness," wrote Gloria, in *Struck By Lightning.* "I had left my home determined to conquer the world, but at what a price! I put my home and my children in second place. I always used to say: if I have beautiful breasts, it is to show them; why hide them? I said the same thing about my legs because I knew I had spectacular legs and nice abdominal muscles. But in an instant, I saw with horror how my whole life had been only a continual and useless care of the body. This was the center of my life: love for my body. And now I no longer had one! The Lord said to me: 'What did you do with the talents I gave you?' Talents? [Treasures?] I came into the world with a mission: that of defending the reign of love. We all have a mission in this world. I saw how the devil is very worried, because the talents that God has placed in us are at the service of the Lord. All of us are worth very much to God. He loves all of us, and each one in a particular way. We all have a mission in this world. But I forgot that I had a soul. I forgot even more to be in the merciful Hands of God. I did not even know that all the good that I had neglected to do had caused much sorrow to Our Lord."

After the beatific vision—after seeing the crystal lakes of Heaven, the structures, the sparkling purity—Dr. Polo found herself in that hideous netherworld of tunnels.

She was shown people she had encountered and then quickly had ignored, people she had been *meant to help.*

She was shown how she had analyzed everything from the aspect of money.

Now, her "pockets" had nothing in them. "Spiritual treasures?" she lamented. "My hands were empty!"

It was just her with the Lord and the Book of Life.

When a Baptist army veteran from Michigan named Marvin J. Besteman went to the threshold of eternity after pancreatic surgery, it was literally that: an entrance, past which were likewise the volumes of life. As Besteman, a banker, pointed out, the New Testament mentions the "Book of Life" seven times in the Book of Revelation—which like near-death visions depicts streets of "pure gold, as it were, transparent glass" (21:18) and light ("the glory of God") infusing and emanating from all things. The dead are judged, says *Revelation* 20:11-12, "according to what they had done as recorded in the books."

To hear him tell it:

"When I got inside the massive doorway into Heaven, there was an area I can best describe as an inner gate. It was like the ones we read about in Scripture, like the ancient gates that still exist in some parts of the world that have been inhabited for many centuries.

"As my eyes swept from the left to the right, I saw a long shelf that extended about ten to twelve feet in either direction before sort of fading away in a kind of haze or mist. Piled on top of this shelf or table made of stones were books upon books upon books, stacked up three to four books high, all along the surface both left and right. The books stacked on top were about as thick as the Grand Rapids phone book, about two and a half inches. They were bound in what appeared to be ancient black cowhide, worn and antiqued, yet not falling apart at the seams. Like the stones, the books had the patina of ancient day, yet I knew somehow they were stronger and longer-wearing than any books on earth. I can't tell you what language the book was written in, whether it was English, Aramaic, or some celestial language only written and read in Heaven."

Where some see their life stories that way, there are those others who view it as that "movie" or incredibly rapid slide show or a series of holograms and whatever the case (the Holy Spirit shows us things in a way we understand, and with images that make us most comfortable: bubbles, trees), the point remains that everything we do on earth is indelible until we are purged; until we are forgiven.

That forgiveness comes in the same volume as we have forgiven others.

It is in the same measure.

"I could see stars lined up suddenly like a curtain," said a young woman named Erica whose organs had been mortally damaged by dependency on a medical drug. "The curtain opened slowly. It was my life review. It was God and me in a big 'movie theatre.' That's when my life review began, and literally for me the life review was from the day I was born up to the day when I had taken my last breath and died. In this life review I was shown everything from things like losing my first tooth, graduating from high school. I saw what man deems important accomplishments—awards I had won at athletics or cheerleading. It was all in chronological order and I was viewing it as if I was in the same room and it was the first time it happened. As we're observing it, I'm living it. And we finally get to the end and I knew to look down and a pair of eyeglasses appeared in front of me. I put them on and I could see, I could really see, with God's Eyes and the curtain opened again and this time I didn't see it like the first time, but from God's view. This time it was the things that were important to God—and they were not at all the accomplishments I had seen before. These were things like love and acts of kindness: befriending somebody who everyone was mean to, helping an animal, giving money to a homeless person when I really didn't have money to give, helping an elderly person across a street—every single thought, word, and action was all about love and we relived them like the first time. I felt so much unconditional love from God as we relived those events together. As soon as the life review was over I knew to look up and this was the only time I was able to see God, from His Shoulder down to His Fingertips, and His Arm was bigger than a semi-truck and I remember Him motioning me to look up and I looked as high as the brightest stars and I looked at the Palm of His Hands and in His Hand appeared a rock and I watched Him unleash the rock and we watched it fall together and it seemed like it took forever and He said, 'I am the Rock and I am the Light,' and as He said this the rock was bright—blinding bright—yet I could watch it and in front of me appeared a body of water, the largest ocean you could imagine, and we watched this rock fall into the ocean and it made one single ripple and we watched the ripple grow and grow and grow until you couldn't even see the borders of that ripple and God said, 'You are the rock. You are the light. You are the ripple that affects mankind.' I knew from the two life reviews what that meant: It meant each and every one of us being that 'rock' while we're on this personal journey and we affect every other person."

Your uniqueness is your value and your value is your contribution on this earthly journey.

We work together with different gifts.

We are not light unless we love others.

"While I was enveloped by the Light, I knew the answers to the questions that had formulated in my mind," said Elane Durham of Libertyville, Illinois. "I knew the answers to the questions that I had formulated in my mind. Secrets from the beginning of time to infinity were clear to me. Myriads of things were understandable. I understood, for example, that when I left earth I would leave with whatever spiritual growth I had attained there, and I would take that spiritual growth with me into this new world."

The Lord wants us to return with the gifts He has given us—the gifts He gives us all, the ones particular to us and our missions.

We must be quiet and listen to receive them.

They are tainted by ego, self-righteousness, and bitterness.

This emphasizes the importance not just of *forgiving*, but forgetting (or at least trying one's best).

Forgiving begins the healing; forgetting completes it. God just wants your best effort.

Another man entered the eternal realm with a "board" on which his life and all he had done (and not done) were etched. Yet one more, a middle-aged woman, saw her life on a television. You are you and you are those you affected. You feel both. You will love the moments of kindness and compassion.

Kindness and *compassion.*

Love purifies all.

The deepest love is not just making others feel good (though this is very often part of it) but often also challenging, correcting, and purging those around us: correcting when correction goes to the benefit of a soul (as opposed to causing discouragement, which is what an angry admonition most often does). It is not being high-handed; it is being concerned. It is cooperating instead of competing. It is using religion to benefit salvation—not just as a "legal" precaution for the afterlife (though God does reward diligence; though He certainly notes obedience).

What do you not want in your suitcase?

Have you asked Christ to help you remove it?

Have you dedicated Communion to reparation?

Have you asked for an illumination of conscience (especially during Mass)?

(Our Blessed Mother often helps in this way!)

There are those who believe mankind will some day collectively experience such an "illumination." An event will occur that will allow people to see themselves "in the burning fire of Divine Truth," as one writer put it, as if standing before a mirror of veracity or looking at an "x-ray" of the soul. It will have to do, some believe, with an event in the sky. If a comet suddenly appeared in the noonday sky, with no idea where it would go, just hanging there, for all the networks to broadcast, and us to see, it would cause each of us to search inwardly! It reminds us of sun miracles such as those at Fatima. Might they be foreshadows? A mystic in 1825 foresaw a "great light" that would come as a sign of reconciliation between man and God. Another said that "a great purification will come upon the world preceded by an 'illumination of conscience' in which everyone will see themselves as God sees them." Some prophesy a "miniature judgment" upon the world. It will be a sign, a grace, and a punishment, depending on one's state. It will last a short time. A warning. Perhaps, a series of warnings. It will be like a revelation of our sins, seen both by believers and non-believers. We know for sure this happens after this life. "The sins of the reprobate shall be seen by all at a glance, as in a picture," Saint Basil once said of what we will encounter on the other side. Yet, things we don't commonly take to be failings will be shown along with the obvious ones.

The Book of Life is a book of love (not a legal document).

"The pride of scrupulosity fixes our attention on wrong things, so that we pay exclusive attention to what does not merit such attention, while we are unscrupulous in things which ought to concern us," says a marvelous little meditation called "The Seven Capital Sins." "Pharisaical pride leads us to boastfulness and the criticism of others. It makes us over-talkative; it leads to lies and contradictions. It manifests itself by a legalism in our actions, causing us to fulfill our duties without spirit, but with hypocrisy.

"We may have a pride of spiritual vanity, imagining ourselves to be perfect and our acts always virtuous or finding a thousand reasons to diminish their gravity or excuse our faults when we do not acknowledge them. *Pride is the greatest of sins* because it is the summit of self-love and is directly opposed to submission to God. 'From pride all perdition took its beginning' (*Tobit* 4:14).

"There is a species of pride in every sin, whatever may be the individual nature of the sin itself. Pride was the first sin committed. It was the sin of Lucifer. It was also the root of the Original Sin committed by Adam and Eve. Pride is the most dangerous of sins, because it blinds our understanding, and unless something finally makes us realize the truth, we are liable to go on, day after day, in a spiritual self-delusion, imagining our acts to be good and virtuous when certain habits actually may be vicious.

"When we are blinded by pride, we do not consider our talents and abilities as God's gifts to us, but attribute our good qualities to ourselves, with the right to use them as we see fit."

How many of us can claim to be entirely free of this imperfection?

How many of us are diligent in watching for it daily?

This is what life is: a glorious, daily, minute-to-minute battle against the flesh. See it that way and half the battle is won. Joy comes even with struggle. There will be impatience thrown before you; discard the temptation. There will be lust tossed on your path; discard the temptation. There will be anger. Throw it to the side. There will be critical thoughts; forget it.

Through discipline train yourself to turn criticality into thoughts of sympathy. Pray for a person as soon as he or she enters your thoughts. Put on Erica's "glasses." Don't be discouraged that wrong inclinations repeat; the war is relentless, unto death. Find joy in the challenge. Don't hover over the times you've failed. Try your utmost not to repeat them. See future victory. From joy comes energy. Look at every problem as a potential victory; every opponent as an opportunity (to grow).

There is an inclination to jealousy; rid of it. There is a wave of resentment; root it out. There is morbidity; sweep this from your mind, entirely. Don't be stuck in the past.

Don't get trapped in nostalgia.

The constant requirement: discipline.

Through discipline, you purify.

Through discipline, you pray.

Through discipline, you take custody of your thoughts ("head chatter").

Failures repented are *lessons.*

"Those souls are the quickest to enter Heaven who quickly sense their sins, who are not obstinately taken up by their own self-conceit," said an anonymous 1931 revelation from Germany called "The Secrets of Purgatory: Reminisces of a Soul in Purgatory" (and bearing an imprimatur).

"God judges us, not according to our failings, but according to our good will.

"A soul who is always ready to recognize God's Will and to do it is indeed by that very fact good. Such a soul does not quickly take offense when somebody reminds it of its failings, and tries in a spirit of great joy, pleasure, and gratitude to overcome and lay aside this or that fault. The building built entirely upon self collapses, because it was not constructed on a foundation of humility.

"Humility is the basis for all graces, yes, for our entire lives."

Always consider others at least as good as you are.

It is safest to consider them better.

Bow equally before the mighty and meek.

Without humility there is no way to reconcile with God.

Yet, maintain your dignity.

We block what He sends when we build an ego around us.

"The souls in purgatory are enveloped, as it were, in a thick shroud into which they have wound themselves while living on earth," said that 1931 revelation.

"It is the garment of their own egoism.

"Their main care in this life was themselves, just as the world's highest ideal is self-glorification and honor. It is this which fashions that coarse garment through which the Light of God can hardly penetrate. Many souls on earth do not seriously ask themselves the question: 'Does my way of living please God?' Instead they think without anxiety that their lives are upright and most praiseworthy, but they are mistaken. Indeed, there are even people who gladly go to church, who pray and perform works of mercy—but a thin hard crust forms around their souls. They think that everything they undertake is very pleasing to God. But they never truly seek God's wishes. They perform all their actions without love. There are also souls in purgatory who had great wisdom and learning in this life, who were famous, who did much good for their fellow men, who upheld all righteousness and justice. However, they performed these actions because of ambitious motives. They were entirely permeated with the spirit of the world, living a selfish and independent life, while completely ignoring their Lord and Creator.

"These souls enter eternity with the least knowledge of God. On earth they were well-versed in everything; now they find themselves in the greatest quandaries. Formerly they were so highly educated and now they know nothing, for God reveals the truly great things only to the humble. Such 'wise' men often have shallow souls. They frequently remain a long time in purgatory—until they have been liberated from their ego, until they are aroused from their slumber, until they lose all concern for themselves. They lie, dead and lifeless, in their shroud until Light Everlasting finally penetrates through their windings to the interior. These are the most helpless souls, for they have so much of the world and self in them.

"Souls who were pious and devout on earth on account of the esteem they thereby received from men suffer the pains of purgatory for a long time.

"*Yet*, God alone knows the hearts of His creatures. God alone judges correctly. Yet God is wondrously gentle and kind in His judgments while we, on the contrary, are so hard and blunt. The Lord is unjust to no one. As Judge He is so tender, so loving, so righteous! Everyone who is of good will is dealt with most kindly."

Chapter 9

At times, in His Mercy, God allows our failings to manifest in physical disorder (including illness) to show us the right path. A person "full of himself" may be obese. A "big head" may be plagued by migraines. Ego can cause infection.

When there are "good acts" done for the wrong reasons, the bottom falls out of the suitcase.

Hardness of heart can lead to hardened arteries.

Think of the expression, "He has done well for himself." That means self-aggrandizement.

This we must atone for.

The Lord grants us what we need; the devil gives luxury.

When we seek to be sleek, to showcase ourselves, as icons, when we carry trophies, we are wasting time and God has designed your life so that there is not a single wasted thing. He is perfect—frivolous with nothing. "He has ordained a holy purpose, a duty, a plan for every moment of our lives, and we must fulfill all these intentions of His," said the

German message. "We must give an account of every minute."

Despise no one; care not if you are despised. Be direct and simple.

The more we die to "self," the more we are born into Heaven.

"Love, humility, and abandonment to God are the three golden keys to going directly to Heaven," noted the writer of a little book about an alleged mystic named Maria Simma of Austria who claimed to see souls from purgatory and who when asked what was the most dangerous to bring to the threshold of death said, "sins against charity, against the love of one's neighbor, hardness of heart, hostility, slandering, calumny, all these things." Once asked about a certain man and woman who'd died, the mystic claimed the man, a strong churchgoer, but critical—harsh, always besmirching—was still expiating in purgatory while the woman, who'd died during an abortion, had been released due to humility and true repentance.

When you spot someone with failings, see them the way they one day can be. Pray them to be that. Look in the mirror. When you spot someone who is not hygienic, perhaps a homeless person, see them like God sees them: as potentially immaculate. One day you may well see them like that in Heaven. Their task, their learning experience, is hygiene. Others are challenged by their tempers, lack of education, caustic personalities, inclinations to drink, sloth, or atheism. View them like they were as infants. We must never assume the role of judge. You may know where someone is but not how they got there, what burdens they carry, what spirits they battle, nor where they will end. Put kindness and loyalty in your chest pocket (next to your heart).

Forsake what is material.

"If one wishes to receive a full indulgence at the moment of death—that means going straight to Heaven—the soul has to be free from all attachment," Maria also asserted.

Will you be able to take your Armani suit? Would you *want* to wear an Armani suit (now seeing the brilliant robes of spun light)? Can you drive a Mercedes to Heaven?

What is beautiful to the world is often ugly in the spirit.

We try and fail to imitate the hereafter with gold, jewels, and flashy mansions. A resemblance, yes—but a faint one!

"Cascading . . . majestic . . . and throwing of rainbows in their mighty mist," are the living waters.

Above, a luminosity far larger than the northern lights, infinitely so, undulates without end.

We could never duplicate the sights of Heaven.

I knew a man named Ned Dougherty who "died" during a fight outside the nightclub he owned in the Hamptons on Long Island (home to the super-rich). Ned had a second club in West Palm Beach, and lived the life of limos, models, celebrities, Dom Perignon champagne, and seaplanes. On July 2, 1984, something happened to him, something like a heart attack or a stroke, and Dougherty found himself collapsing on the sidewalk outside his club after a fist fight with an associate. Suddenly, he felt like he was "floating, suspended in a black, bottomless pit."

In the distance he could hear voices. "No vitals! We're losing him!" said an emergency technician in an ambulance en route to the hospital.

Dougherty was able to sit up in the spirit, rise above the ambulance, and watch it speed off. As he was suspended in the air he saw a "kaleidoscopic review" of his life and possessions, which then vaporized.

Again suddenly, a mass of energy formed and shaped itself into a cylinder funneling skyward.

Drawn into another realm, Ned was enveloped by the Light of God. There was "symphonic" music. There were buildings made of nothing earthly. There were spirits: hundreds upon hundreds of relatives were there, as in an amphitheatre. In the review of his life he was made to understand the relationship he'd had with his father, who had been an alcoholic. He understood why certain people did and felt as they had and how it had affected him and he had affected others. It was an assessment. He understood himself. It was also a conviction: of his obsession with money. He was presented a mission that focused on charity and returned to earth, where he soon forsook the luxuries to which he had grown accustomed, as well as his own drinking (becoming an evangelist).

Those who come back disdain material accomplishments. There was Don Brubaker, who found himself plunging in a dark tunnel in the presence of Satan, who told him he could avoid all pain and anguish and have anything he liked if he would just follow him. "Visions of wealth appeared before my eyes," said Don, "like a three-dimensional movie. Diamonds, money, cars, gold, beautiful women, everything. I was overwhelmed by the vision. I could almost touch it, it seemed so real."

A visionary once saw the devil as an extremely handsome man who offered the seer "happiness in life and love" if she would follow him (instead of the Blessed Mother).

What Mary said, when *she* appeared, was that if we are close enough to her we may have our trials on earth, but we won't even feel the passage of death.

On the other hand, an obsession with something material can detain a soul to a purgatory on earth, if not worse.

"When my spirit began to leave my body I began to go down into a very deep pit," said a woman named Christine Eastell, who had left Christianity, at least in an active way.

"It is difficult to describe. It was very black and misty. There was no beginning or end, and no sides. I just knew it was a pit. It was black but something worse than black. I can't describe it because it's not like black is to us, of this world. There were no sides, there was no back, front, top, bottom. It was just a black bottomless pit. I was traveling down this pit and there were people everywhere and they were walking around with such torment on their faces, their shoulders stooped as if everything bad in the world was on them. It was the most dreadful experience. Even recounting it I can still feel that pain, that torture, torment. I kept shutting my eyes, thinking, 'You're only dreaming,' but no!, I wasn't. Every time I opened them, it didn't change at all. It was still that intense despair. I was quite hysterical at this point and in the background I could feel not just despair but a depth of despair, an evil. I looked up and spiritually I knew I was in the presence of Satan, I knew I was given a glimpse of hell. When I saw what I thought was a small opening I began to claw desperately. But the more I tried to get to this opening, the more distant it became. That is what I know happened to me. I said, 'I'm a Christian, I've been to church, I've led a good life, there's no way I should be here, I've done everything that I was supposed to do,' but this voice said to me, 'When I tempted you with worldly things, with success, you chose that way, you stopped going to church, you stopped listening to where you should be, and you belong to me!' At that point I just got down on my knees and pleaded with Jesus to rescue me."

He did. And took her to a place of "pure love, joy, hope, peace.

"Jesus was in front of me surrounded by a light so bright," she recalled, "you couldn't look into His Face."

Said a man named Bill Wiese who had a similar vision, "As I stood near that enormous pit of fire, no immediate attackers seemed to be threatening, so this gave me a moment to take in my surroundings. It was raining fire and burning rock, similar to the way lava falls from the sky when a volcano explodes. The smoke from the flames was very thick, allowing visibility for only a short distance, but what I could see was horrifying. I saw many people reaching out of the pit of fire, desperately trying to claw their way out. But there was no escape. I turned my head, and I noticed that I was standing in the middle of a cave. The wall wrapped around me and led to the vast expanse of the pit. As I looked at the walls, I saw that they were covered with thousands of hideous creatures. These demonic creatures were all sizes and shapes. Some of them had four legs and were the size of bears. Others stood upright and were about the size of gorillas. They were all terribly grotesque and disfigured. It looked as though their flesh had been decomposing and all their limbs were twisted and out of proportion. To the right of the large inferno were thousands of small pits, as far as I could see. Each pit was no more than three to five feet across and four to five-feet deep—each pit holding a single lost soul."

We recall *Psalm* 94:13: ". . . until the pit is dug for the wicked."

Richard Eby described a similar vision in which he was placed in a pit with spider-like demons.

The conversion of a famous preacher named Kenneth E. Hagin came when "on the twenty-first day of April, 1933, 7:30 p.m., at McKinney, Texas, my heart stopped beating and the spiritual man that lives in my body departed from my body . . . I went down, down, down, down, until the lights of the earth faded away . . . The further down I went the blacker it became, until it was all blackness. I could not have seen my hand if it had been one inch in front of my eyes. The further down I went, the more stifling it was and the hotter it was."

These visions were given so they would come back and remind people—including God's faithful—that hell exists.

It reflects what is in us.

It is as dark as what we have done.

It is as hot as it needs to be to burn off what is around us.

It inspires us—hearing such accounts—to cleanse every aspect of our lives.

"This is the way my life was reviewed," said a registered nurse named Grace Bubulka, who went to the threshold of death during a miscarriage. "I was deeply aware and had profound insight into everything in my life and all of my dealings with others from my birth on to the moment of my near-death experience. All those in the light were witness to this review of my entire life. I was enveloped in a loving feeling and given insight into areas of my life that were not compatible with eternity in the light. I also knew now how to correct this. I was charged with the accountability of the remainder of my life. I knew that more was ahead in the light that continued forever but I could not go there now. Seeing my life left me with the impression that my life mattered and was somehow significant as to how far I could go into the light. My work was not yet finished and my work was to begin inside me and within my family."

Are you in chains—or are you a "chain-*breaker*"?

This is a relevant question because every person and couple and family has its fetters, its iron shackles, its handcuffs, its manacles. It's part of your mission to shed these.

No doubt you sense right away what this refers to: traits and proclivities and things that constrain us, that bind us up, that stop us, that halt forward progress, that remove our freedom, that cast us into the darkness, sometimes, of a dungeon. We are successful but we are not successful. We are happy but we are not happy. We are at peace but not really. What holds you back? What frustrates you? What keeps repeating? Where do you always find a roadblock? Make a list. Often, it's a simple matter of having a strong will. That's a prerequisite: to succeed in this place of adversity called earth you must have an inner will that perseveres—as the Old Testament (*Psalms*) puts it, a "right" and "steadfast" spirit. *I'll never get that job,* you might be fretting. *I'll never finish this work. I'll never make this or that trip—never get there. I'll never find the right spouse. I'll never . . .*

That's a wrong spirit. We get into such ruts when we should be "breaking" the bondage by saying the opposite (*I will get there, I will get the right job . . .*), waking up every morning, as a preacher once said, and deciding to be happy, deciding to have a good day (delighting even in its trials). And at the end of the day, we should thank God even if we haven't received what we want, because (be it His Will) the end of the day means we are another day closer to the desire of our hearts. "God meets us," he notes, "at the level of our expectations."

To do that takes an iron will because it is only iron that's strong enough to break iron shackles. Adversity is a gift that allows us to "pump iron," to build spiritual muscle. When we do all we can in the natural, God performs the supernatural. Be strong. Be determined. If you're not, you won't see miracles, you won't reach your full potential, which means you will fall short of your mission. You are only happy when you are moving to completion of your assignment on this earth. When we have an "iron will" we also have *free* will because an iron will breaks bondages. It makes the soul patient when the issue is impatience; calm when the issue is anxiety; humble when the issue is pride. Whatever your fault is, just will yourself not to repeat it (use that muscle). Are you angry? Just stop being angry. Force the issue. Are you slothful? Be diligent. Just do it! List negative traits in your life and lineage and then simply don't repeat them. Only in freedom can you get back to who you really are. You don't want to be "bound on the way to Babylon" (*2 Chronicles* 33:11). Don't wait for things to make you happy. Get happy before anything happens and God will make you happier yet. ("Shake yourself from the dust, rise up, O captive Jerusalem; Loose yourself from the chains around your neck, O captive daughter of Zion," says *Isaiah* 52:2).

There are chains when we are caught in wrong emotions, when we can't seem to find peace, when there's constant fretting, when there are addictions. We're in bondage when we are obsessed with anyone or anything; our focus can't expand to a wider landscape. We may even be in chains that involve illness passed down through the family line and other such serious physical, emotional, or spiritual problems. And so we repeat the question: do you want to continue that pattern—just "go with the flow"—or disrupt it, get out of the flow, when the flow is heading toward Niagara?

It is best to be a chain-breaker. If there is anything in your family line that has wrapped chains around you or members of your household, break those shackles in the Name of Jesus. Set out on the "right course." Get to freedom of will.

Your purpose in life is met when your spirit is free.

It's so easy to be in that wrong "groove." Many times, members of families don't spiritually grow because it becomes *Groundhog Day*: constantly the same thing, the same negativities, the same conversations, day in and day out. The ball is not moving forward. There is a broken record, stagnation, and when there is stagnation, it is a swamp. The flow of water stops. We are "closed in." We know how much snakes like swamps. Just one person bound in chains can pass darkness around and disrupt, even destroy, a household.

Ridding ourselves of negative traits we "inherited" is to do the Will of God. It doesn't mean isolation. It doesn't mean separation. It certainly doesn't mean antagonism. It means moving forward with one's chief focus and affinity: God. To break chains is to do the opposite of what binds us; it is to reconstruct; it means diligence. It means self-honesty. It also means right loyalty. You break bonds when God is your key relationship.

"We face the choice every day," noted one author. "In every difficulty we can choose to create something new and healthy or to recycle the poison of generations past. We can send our children on to their own children with backgrounds of love and kindness and patience, or we can deliver them over to the same hells we may have received from our own parents."

We face this choice every day. Never mind yesterday. Every day, start fresh (with that joy). As another preacher advises: where there is sin, repent; where bitterness has taken root, forgive; where there are lies in the fabric of your life, seek truth; where there are poor examples (and bad traditions) start fresh. (*Bad traditions.* Mull that over.) What's the most hurtful emotion or habit you have? Do you keep it close to your chest even though it's a "hot coal"—anger, guilt, impatience? Few chains are as strong as guilt! Were not saints chain-breakers? Monk and spiritual writer Albert Holtz related a story of wandering the streets of Toledo, Spain, and encountering an interesting sight at the monastery church of San Juan de los Reyes: way up there on the outside wall, in neat rows, were curious ironwork objects about a foot-and-a-half long. They were ankle chains taken off of Christian slaves freed from their Moslem captors who ruled this Spanish city for over 360 years. As Holtz himself said, "What more appropriate trophies for Christians than the broken chains of their former captivity? And what better place to display such trophies than on the side of a church? After all, God became flesh, suffered, died, and rose again to free humanity from all that enslaved us. We are no longer slaves to evil, doubt, and despair, because God has loosed our bonds."

"God is in the business of breaking chains," says the preacher.

What chains are in your life? In your family's? Why not list them. And why not bring that list to Confession and the Eucharist. Why not Plead the Blood of Jesus to break them when the priest elevates the mighty chalice?

If you go to the Holy Spirit, He will enlighten you as to whether a block in your life is His way of turning you in another direction or it is from a personal defect (or spirit) that stymies you on the way to happiness. When you have done all that is possible, He will come to do the *im*possible.

You stray from your mission when you're selfish, when you do something for show (instead of to serve others), when you have the wrong kind of ambition. This brings a darkness that can be detected even on earth around people who need our prayers. The darker they are, the more they must draw power. Their own energy has been blocked. A "well" has been plugged. They drain us. The connection to the Living Waters, to the *manna* of God, has busted; they must sap energy from others. There is no Light.

In the afterlife, this becomes totally obvious.

We *wear* our darkness.

Great darkness comes when there is indifference to Him Who created us.

"In Heaven, they love Him very much, there He is compensated," said that nun in the French revelation called *An Unpublished Manuscript on Purgatory*.

"He wants to be loved on earth, on that earth where He annihilates Himself in every tabernacle, in order to be approached more easily and yet He is refused."

"Alas, how many lives seem to be filled with good works and at death are found empty. This is because all those actions that appeared to be good, all those showy works, all that conduct that seemed irreproachable—all these were not done for Jesus alone. Some will have their eyes opened when they come to purgatory. On earth they wanted to be made much of, to shine, to be thought very exact in religious observances, to be esteemed as perfect religious. This is the mainspring of so many lives. If you only knew how few people work for God and act for Him alone: Alas, at death, when they are no longer blinded, what regrets they will have. If only sometimes they would think of eternity. What is life compared to that day which will have no evening for the elect, or to that night which will have no dawning for the damned? On earth, people attach themselves to everything and everyone except to Him, Who alone ought to have our love and to Whom we refuse it. Jesus in the tabernacle waits for souls to love Him and He finds none. Hardly one soul in a thousand loves Him as it should."

Chapter 10

And so there can be a disconnection. We go to eternity with less than we can. We see this with those who suffer from a "spirit of religiosity," folks who are legalistic and follow the rules—on the surface, a holy life—but too often had been harsh on others, fixated on the parts, the mechanics, instead of the spirit; not using the gifts of the Church properly. They genuflect correctly but have exhibited a wrong heart.

They can tell you the difference between blessed and chrism oils. They have the holy days memorized: all good things.

But if it doesn't lead to love (only to self-righteousness, even spiritual arrogance, which becomes judgmentalism), such people, in their zeal, and scrupulosity, are fooling themselves.

Rosary after rosary must be applied properly. They must lead us upward.

It is not a routine. If you pray by rote—automatically, with no feeling—reform your prayer. If you harbor ill will, correct this as soon as you can (by imploring the Holy Spirit).

At Kibeho, the Lord allegedly told a seer, when asked why religious misunderstandings and disunity occur, *"It is because they believe without believing; they love without loving."*

A prayer from the heart is almost inconceivably powerful when it is well-intended, unselfish, seeks to cleanse, and asks for what the soul needs (such as a virtue) instead of what the body and mentality and sensuality desire. Prayers for a virtue are virtually always answered.

A truly spiritual person has love and expresses love through humility, which can come from the Rosary, for was not Mary humble?

When there's haughtiness that is a blaring sign that says, "Arrogance. No Love." When there is superiority, it is loving oneself above those over whom we feel superior.

Again, this is peril. I must emphasize and re-emphasize it: An attitude of superiority has no place in Heaven. We don't know exactly where we stand with God until He shows us (which He will do gently, lovingly, but in a way of truth that's impossible to deny) our lives, from His perspective.

God evaluates right back to the very beginning of our ancestries. He knows what we were born with. He knows how we were raised. He knows our handicaps. He knows what we're supposed to do. He knows how we're supposed to progress. He knows what genetic or psychological or spiritual baggage a person has. He knows the angels and demons, the disembodied, that may be inhibiting us.

A haughty spirit indeed goes before a fall!

"There are souls in purgatory, even religious, who have very much to suffer because of their sham and feigned piety," said the 1931 revelation from Germany. "Men who have real, genuine piety are always discreet and understanding, because they are intimately united with the Holy Spirit and therefore harm no one. *This is why there is correct judgment.* The discreet are never harsh or bitter; they can understand everyone, even sinners. Each soul appears like a beautiful mosaic made by God with a marvelous Divine art and consisting of many little stones. All the graces which we possess God has worked into this masterpiece. If we destroy or lose these tiny mosaic stones, if we do not continually endeavor to beautify this mosaic in our souls, we cause such ugly gaps. In purgatory this picture must be completed; everything that had been lost must be restored so that nothing is wanting to the soul's original splendor. God Himself—the wonderful God—would be outraged if all were not restored. The souls which enter Heaven must lack for nothing.

"The sufferings and trials on earth are meritorious; do not lose one of them," said that nun in "Unpublished Manuscript." "But above all, love. Love wipes out many faults and makes one avoid them so as not to give pain to the One we love."

All our lives we must "pack our bags" with love for God.

This is the single greatest key to eternity.

If we love Him with our whole hearts, Heaven encircles us, even now.

The test of life is a test of love.

Everything is love and is about love.

Love is the bridge to our true being.

Look at the devil: a total lack of love.

It is what defines him.

It also defines us.

Cherish others and you will be cherished to the core of your being by God.

"One of the many beliefs I have formed from [my near-death] experience is that whenever unconditional love is bestowed upon an individual, no matter what the strength or from what source (a person or the Light), it causes a purging of 'unloving energy' or self-hating energy to come into the consciousness of the individual to be examined and discharged," said another of those death experiencers. "Thus, the individual's level of consciousness is raised every time this is done."

"It takes a while to distill away some of our attitudes and leave it behind," said a man named David recently on YouTube. "I think we bring some of it with us for a while. When we bring intolerance, it must be distilled. I took three immediate lessons. The first was acceptance, because I saw my entire life and I got to see it through other people's perspectives and in such a way that I understood suddenly who I was and I could accept who I was. I may not be a perfect person, but I could accept that and work on it. And I feel that the acceptance was a big lesson, because with acceptance you can be comfortable in your skin, and in that life review I saw I was pretty brash, didn't have much understanding of other people's points of view, and if you didn't agree with my point of view, I didn't care much for you. You weren't much part of my life. In the life review I got to see that there are other people's paths that don't have anything to do with mine and now I have a tolerance I didn't have before because I saw that they may have a path and purpose in life that doesn't necessarily have to agree with mine. We're going to exchange paths, we're going to cross paths, and we're going to interact and many times I may not agree with their personal views or what they're doing or what they want to achieve in life, but that's all right. I think in a lot of life's interactions we need to enjoy the good and the bad. There are people who are going to push our buttons and they can be teachers to us. I've learned to accept myself and accept others. When my heart sings I know it is my truth. A lot of us have passions that we repress in life and I think after an experience you tend not to suppress that because it's another indicator of the interaction that we're going through in life and a way to squeeze all the juice from an interaction so that you can learn from it."

One woman who had an "illumination of conscience" wrote me:

"Back in 1991 at age thirty, I came down with a mysterious and painful illness that doctors couldn't diagnose. They agreed I had many symptoms that could be linked to a variety of ailments, among them multiple sclerosis, lupus, etcetera. But they couldn't say for sure what the problem was, and prescribed medicines for the main symptoms, which were unremitting pain and stiffness.

"Unfortunately the pain didn't go away and the medicines didn't work. Over a period of two and a half years, I became increasingly depressed as I became unable to work. Doctors began to suggest that my pain and other symptoms were all 'in my head' since they were unable to diagnose me. I began to consider trying to end my own life, which until then I had lived only for my own pleasure and wants. Around this time, I began to read the Gospels at length. I didn't plead with God to cure me as I had before, but instead, for the first time, I was more concerned with reading about the spiritual promises of God and in finding out more and more about His great love for us and His plan for our lives and eternity. While I wasn't yet a Christian and had not been baptized, I wanted to know Jesus and make a change in the way I had been living.

"I went to the public library and checked out books on comparative religion and spirituality. I prayed every day for a long time, often late into the night, as my husband was working in another state at the time and I only had myself to look after. For about eight months I lived this way, only leaving the house to visit family, go to the library, grocery shop, and attend Mass. One night in October of 1993, I cleaned up the kitchen, got a cup of tea, and settled down for my nightly devotional reading. I was about two hours into it and reading in the Books of Acts, *Romans*, and others parts of the Gospels and also was reading excerpts from a book called *The Prophet*. I remember crying because of the beauty of the words, when I heard a noise, like a mini-explosion in the kitchen, and a sound of something shattering.

"In the kitchen, I saw a heavy glass that I used as a pencil holder in fragments on the countertop, broken into curious little squares. I checked the windows, walls, and doors for a possible projectile that could've caused the glass to shatter (there had been occasional drive-by shootings in the vicinity of my home recently), but nothing. Feeling a little anxious, I went to bed and fell asleep after a long prayer. For the first time ever, I prayed that His Will would be done in my life rather than my own. I slept deeply, which was somewhat unusual.

"All of a sudden, I was awakened by a very sharp blow to the left side of my neck. It cracked my neck over to one side, and I heard myself say 'Owww!' as if from a distance or down a long tube. Immediately or perhaps simultaneously a really loud noise sounding like a door slamming (but seeming every bit as loud as a sonic boom) came from a direction in the room where there was neither a door nor a window. The room shook. I was shocked and awake when I began to seemingly leave my physical body and rise. I do not have a very clear memory of exactly all that transpired while I was in this 'altered state.' I say 'altered' because I don't know for sure whether I was truly awake, asleep, or something else! I was mentally alert because I remember certain things very clearly but I was not using my eyes much to see. In fact most of my memories are of emotions and impressions, not of things seen actually as one sees them in the world.

"One of the things I know clearly is that I was ascending into the air outside my physical body. Creatures were in the air with me—I have the impression now that they were angels—but I can't clearly remember. They were saying things to me, seemingly imparting information, and there was music. I looked up and saw a star or light above me. This star or light was huge and blindingly brilliant, but the main characteristic of it was that it was pouring out *love*. The love coming out of that star was overwhelming and like nothing I had ever experienced. It made me acutely aware of how small my own ability to love was, drowned in the ocean of this great Love like a grain of sand. I knew that at all costs, I wanted to go to the Light which I was sure was God's dwelling place.

"So I did. I ascended faster and faster, and at some point I stopped ascending under my own power, because the star was actually pulling me in. The closer I got to the light of the star, the more the love poured out upon me. Finally, in a great burst of joy, the light seemed to fill me completely up and began to pour out of me. I felt like I had grown to one hundred feet tall, and a song was pouring out of me along with the light. I felt like I had known this song forever, but it certainly wasn't in English—I was singing in a tongue that felt much more familiar than English (which is my mother tongue). The song was a hymn praising God, but I can't tell you now what the words were. The strange thing was that the song was coming not out of my throat, but seemingly out of every single cell in my body!

"I cannot accurately describe the extreme bliss of that moment. Rapture would be a good word for it. Suddenly, something shocking happened. All at once, I began to burn. It felt like I was in a fire which was consuming me entirely. I thought to myself that I was surely about to be annihilated, and a pang of fear struck me. And then the strange thought came to me: that I didn't care, that I loved God so much that it was okay by me if he wiped me out of existence forever. I saw my absolute dependence on God and that I was helpless in His Hands. He could kill me or let me live, whichever He wanted and I just didn't care, as long as I could be in the Presence of that love of His until my last conscious thought."

Chapter 11

Love through discipline. To have discipline is to be a disciple. Things will come to you on the path of your life. Your heart must design that path.

When He nudges, take note of it.

When He pushes, take note of it.

When He whispers, listen.

When He shouts, heed it!

If there is one over-riding consistency among stories of the afterlife, it's the incredible, indescribable, brilliant Love emanating from Heaven.

We must take our own love and join it with His.

"Jesus, I trust in You. Lord, I surrender to You. I place everything—all—in Your Hands."

The more faith and love we have, the higher and brighter a place there will be. You will "graduate" upward according to the light you emanate.

Those who come closest to being able to abandon with a full heart will have the easiest path to the lofty places.

There is the initial countryside. There are meadows. There are gardens. There are mountains. There are cities of light—the higher spheres.

Those who get to those highest initial realms are those who have brought much in the way of bettering all life and things.

They are those who sought the knowledge of the Lord.

They are those who completed their missions and now (literally) have a higher calling.

Not everyone in a family will immediately attain the same state.

As Jedediah Grant noted, "To my astonishment, when I looked at families there was a deficiency in some, there was a lack, for I saw families that would not be permitted to come and dwell together, because they had not honored their calling here [on earth]."

But in the afterworld, they'll see each other. They'll visit. They will spend time together - even much time, sometimes in the same abode.

We see those we loved again—this time with no squabbles, with no competitions, in this place where buildings capture the sacredness of the surroundings—where "night" is a simple, partial fading of the glory.

"There, advancing up the long room to meet me, I saw my dear father and mother and with them my youngest sister," wrote Rebecca Springer. "With a cry of joy, I flew into my father's outstretched arms and heard his dear, familiar, 'My precious little daughter!'

"'At last! At last!' I cried, clinging to him. 'At last I have you again!'"

Her brother-in-law led Rebecca to a house he had helped to fashion for his wife, when her time came. "We entered the truly beautiful house, built of the purest white granite, so embedded in the foliage of the flower-laden trees that from some points only glimpses of its fine proportions could be seen," claimed Rebecca. "We passed through several delightful rooms on the lower floor. Then, ascending the stairway—which in itself was a dream of beauty—we entered the room he was so anxious for me to see. I stopped upon the threshold with an exclamation of delight. 'It is the most delightful room I ever saw!' I cried enthusiastically."

In eternity, simply thinking of a dear one brings the presence of that person (if God so allows). In fleeting glimpses, this can also occur on earth. "I've had many experiences with the dead or dying," a woman named Joan Beauregard wrote to me. "This is the only one I have had in which I believe the person attended their own funeral. It was my friend, Carol. Her memorial was held on Padre Island, Texas, at a hotel that was on the beach.

"We were on a back stone patio with a stone surround encompassing the patio. It was high enough and wide enough to sit on comfortably. I was listening to the booming surf as well as the person who was eulogizing her and looking out to sea when I 'saw' a light-person sitting on the surround. No features, just light, but I could make out the way the person was dressed—just like Carol!

"She seemed to be listening. In a few moments, three other luminous beings appeared, one right next to her. When the eulogy became sad, she would disappear, and then reappear when [the eulogist] offered something upbeat about her life. Carol always dwelt on the positive!

"I thought I was really seeing things, but it lasted almost the entire eulogy.

Ellen Perry of Galveston, Texas, told me that "on the Sunday before my mom's death, my husband and I were with her.

"She suddenly sat up in bed and looked upwards. She then laid back down and had the most peaceful look I have ever seen. I hugged her and she hugged me back and took our hands and placed them on her heart. Three times that afternoon, she sat up and reached for someone, then laid back down. We knew something was happening that we could not see. She then went to sleep for three days and took her last breath with us present. A white cross appeared in our daughter's window early the morning of mom's death. She texted it to me knowing it meant mom was going to Heaven that day. Mom said three Rosaries every day until she got Alzheimer's disease. The priest came to the nursing home at nine at night prior to mom's death to anoint her and give her absolution, thus Our Lady kept her promise that apostles of the Rosary will not die without the sacraments. She also died clothed in the Brown Scapular. We are Third Order Carmelites."

I commit my spirit to You, oh God; I love Thee with my whole heart.

These are the best last words.

"We arrived at another realm," said a man named Bob Helm who died during surgery (and found himself in the company of a being in a robe that was brilliant white). "We appeared to be alone there, except for the street-sweeper, who was responsible for the spotless condition of the place. Here again, the colors and textures were outside my experience; and the road and the sidewalks appeared to be paved in some kind of precious metal. The buildings appeared to be constructed of a translucent material. I felt prompted to talk to the street-sweeper and congratulated him on his efforts. He said work was a joy to him, and he derived his pleasure from doing the best job he could at all times."

Said another: "We have only one object set before us: the betterment of all life and all things."

It's said that we choose what age we want to appear as. How do we find our "jobs"—our roles—in Heaven? "Well," an angel supposedly said to a man named John Oxenham, "there are two things we've got to do here: continue our own education for the higher sphere and help those who are needing help, either here or elsewhere or still on earth. And we naturally want to help in the ways we know best."

When we're on that quest, when we seek to please God every moment, when all we do—work, eat, tasks, even spousal relations—are from a spiritual perspective, we are on our way to purgation.

We purge also in how we handle *adversity*.

Trying your best is enough for God. He knows you can't do everything we'd like to. Just try. Make the attempt. Find your mission in what your instinct, your gut, your intuition tells you.

Challenging, "bad" things can be God's greatest gift.

They're often sent to refine—or awaken—us.

What would you do if you were "electrocuted" and lost much of your left arm and leg?

This happened to a man I met named Robert Morales, Junior, of Austin, Texas.

Instead of becoming bitter, he got closer to God—and as a result, became a "miracle-worker."

It was back in 1974 that Morales, in his twenties, was employed as an assistant lineman, when one day he made the mistake of grabbing a live wire and found himself hanging on a tower, helplessly, as 7,200 volts of current surged through him!

Up there, within a whisker of death, he saw the past ten years of his life flash as on a television in front of him.

Robert didn't like what he saw.

His was a life distant from God.

Wisely, he called out to God; repented; and turned his life over to the Lord.

That's all it takes.

"I knew I wasn't right with Him," Robert recounted. "I wasn't going to Mass. I was away from the sacraments. I was searching for the things of this world, not the things of His world. I was going to die up there, and so I called out and gave myself totally to God, let it be His Will whether I lived or died.

"The next thing I knew, there was like an explosion. It threw me backwards and my feet went into the braces that make like a cross up there on the post. Despite how I was living, I always wore some kind of religious medal, and I had one of St. Martin de Porres. The medal came out of my shirt and hit me in the forehead. You can picture me upside-down with this hitting me in the forehead!"

The backward motion and Morale's new position—with a piece of the tower brace now between his feet—broke the circuit. Electricity stopped surging through his body. He was badly damaged (in need of more than a dozen subsequent operations, including amputation), but Robert Morales was alive; reborn; beaming with the love of Jesus.

Returning home from the doctor two months after the "horrible" event, his wife noticed that a wide, perfectly formed cross had appeared on the back rest of his wheelchair.

A second image was also present, resembling a dove.

No one could fathom how they'd gotten there.

Morales started a chapel called *Los Milagros de Cristo* ("The Miracles of Christ") where healings are said to take place.

It was the "hard way," but he had found his mission.

What for most would be a tragedy became the happiest day of his life.

Chapter 12

It is only when we develop a "holy understanding" that we see this. We also see the good in others. We wish misfortune on no one. If we don't want misfortune ourselves, now or later, we should not luxuriate over the ill fortune of others. In such a way is it that (as *Proverbs* also says), "a righteous man falls seven times, and rises again (24:16)" while "the wicked stumble in time of calamity." The "*bigger*" we are, the harder we fall.

The lazier we are, the quicker we plummet.

As ego leaves, your robe brightens.

Darkness leaves.

"He who overcomes will thus be clothed in white garments," says *Revelation* 3:5, ("and I will not erase his name from the Book of Life, and I will confess his name before My Father and before His angels").

The soul must be cleansed by strict control of thoughts. When a person comes to mind, if the automatic reaction is to think of negatives associated with the person, or a lustful inclination (if the imagination immediately takes certain paths), this "program," this broken-record in the thought process, must be banished and the Holy Spirit, in the Name of Jesus, does this: purifies our thoughts, when we ask, so we avoid having to erase them on the other side. Violent thoughts add up in the hereafter, as do loving, joyful ones, and the quality of our afterlives will mirror this. Wrong thoughts must be purged here or in the hereafter.

Saint Mark of Ephesus (an Orthodox saint) said, "If souls have departed this life in faith and love, while nevertheless carrying away with themselves certain faults, whether small ones over which they have not repented at all, or great ones for which—even though they have repented over them—they did not undertake to show fruits of repentance: such souls, we believe, must be cleansed from this kind of sin, but not by means of some purgatorial fire or a definite punishment in some place (for this, as we have said, has not been handed down to us). But some must be cleansed in the very departure from the body."

Confession has to be followed by real change in how we think and act.

Yet, always, there is God's Mercy.

Said the 1931 revelation: "How good God is to permit souls to wipe away such stains in purgatory. Purgatory is therefore temporary suffering. The souls suffer because of time lost. They long inexplicably for God, for purity, for correction; but they are all happy because they know they are in a place of improvement where there is no reason to despair. There, suffering is a hope, a trust, an aspiration, a conversion. God has not given us time in order that we may play with it and do with it as we please. Time is a vessel with which we must draw from the well of life everlasting. Whoever does not bring it back full is made to feel the questioning glance of the Lord Who says: 'What hast thou done with those treasures of Grace? I have commanded thee to bring this vessel back to Me full—and thou hast gone thy own ways, hast forgotten the command of thy God, hast even broken the beautiful, holy vessel. And what dost thou now bring back?'

"Then the soul sinks down before God; it now lies before the Everlasting Judge. It can no longer run away from His Words, as perhaps it did during life. There it lies before the Almighty, returning only fragments to Him—the fragments of so many shattered graces and so much lost time. Then the soul says to God: 'Make it whole again!' If the soul was repentant at death, it will say this with great remorse. Then the Savior is merciful and says: 'Come here! In purgatory we will make it whole again.' But this cannot be done without suffering; for the soul is softened by repentance, and it is by repentance that expiation must be made. But he who brings the vessel back full and unbroken is fortunate beyond measure, for then the gates of eternity stand wide open."

The Baptist army veteran Marvin Besteman encountered an actual "glass-like gate that rose upward and disappeared into a mist" with a multi-colored outline after a massive outer gate that was fashioned with something that resembled the most splendid mahogany.

This is how we enter.

It is the narrow path.

When we're "hard," when we are burgeoning with the goods of the world, with false promises, with wrong goals, with hubris, with intolerance, we must be softened.

Would you put cement in your carry-on? It is a block on your path. It is a block at the gate. It is blindness.

"I had a total, complete, clear knowledge of everything that had ever happened in my life, just everything, which gave me a better understanding of everything at that moment," said another person interviewed for near-death research. "Everything was so clear. I realized that there are things that every person is sent to earth to realize and learn. For instance, to share more love, to be more loving toward one another. To discover that the most important thing is human relationships and love and not materialistic things and to realize that every single thing that you do in your life is recorded and that even though you pass it by not thinking at the time, it always comes up later. For instance, you may be at a stoplight and you're in a hurry and the lady in front of you, when the light turns green, doesn't take right off, doesn't notice the light, and you get upset and start honking your horn and telling them to hurry up. Those are the little kinds of things that are important."

In some way, in some form, usually when you least expect it, the same test will pop up again, if you are prone to fail such tests.

Just try to pass. Just *try* to overcome bad habits.

Just try not to get angry at a slow check-out (or when your computer crashes).

Grace is in the attempt.

Once a fault is rectified, other virtues will flow.

This is God's generosity.

"Follow your love" with patience. It will lead to your secret gifts.

"I should have known!" you will say later, when you review your life. "Of course!" (to reiterate).

Release things you should forgive. Release caring what the world thinks. Release the way others try to form you and disregard them when they try to manipulate or make you guilty. Release guilt. Release trying to do what you are not meant to. You are now freer—freer to move mountains (perhaps start with hills). Your mistake is not taking time to have realization in the moment.

There are things we did and also things we did not do that are reviewed in the hereafter. Dr. Polo said she was taken through her life to a time when she saw a peasant woman crying on television over the body of her slain husband. Instead of praying for the distraught, distressed, and soon destitute woman, Dr. Polo turned to a show on dieting.

This was important to Jesus.

It turned out that the peasant woman was from Dr. Polo's hometown. She was shown the suffering of this woman's family. She felt what it was like when the woman's husband was killed. "In this way, the Lord shows us the pain that He feels and the suffering of others," wrote Polo, "but very often, we interest ourselves only in our own things, and we do not worry about our brothers and their needs! Do you know what the Lord wanted? He wanted me to kneel down and beg Him to help that family! God would have inspired me as to how I could have helped them!"

As Dr. Polo said, "The first thing that we render account to God for are the sins of omission! They are grave. The Lord gave me another opportunity to help her, when years later I saw her again (by this time the woman, forced from her home after the death of her husband, had turned to prostitution). It was a day that I had to go to the center of the city. I detested going there because it is a place of misery and since I felt myself superior, I did not like seeing poverty and things like that. But on that day, I had to go there and while we were passing through, my son asked me: 'Oh! Mamma, why in the world does that lady dress in that way?' I answered him: 'Do not look! These are contemptible women who sell their bodies for pleasure and money: they are prostitutes and are unclean.' Just imagine! To speak like this and poison my son even more. I looked at this sister of mine without pity and she was in this situation because of my indifference!"

It is the devil who desensitizes us to the hardships of others. We say: It's not my problem. Yet, we're all connected; we must pray for everyone—those on TV that day, those you pass on the road, those at the supermarket; the airport; at work; school. When a person irritates us, our prayer immediately should be that they progress beyond the trait that causes us aggravation. When we pray for their improvement, we are no longer irritated. We are part of God's movement.

These prayers are jewels we take to Heaven.

"The Lord showed me how many people suffer in the world and how much I could have helped," wrote the dentist. "Never did I permit the Holy Spirit to touch me, nor did I ever let myself be moved by the suffering of others. The Lord said to me: *'Look at the suffering of my people, look how I needed to wound your family with cancer so that you might be moved for those suffering the same sickness! You were compassionate for the shut-ins only after your husband himself was in that situation.'*

"I was very hypocritical and false. I would speak nicely to peoples' faces, but behind their backs I spoke badly about them. I praised someone saying: 'You are pretty and what a nice dress; it looks very well on you.' But inside I was thinking: 'How gross! You are ugly, and you believe yourself to be the queen!' In the Book of Life, you see all of this. All of my lies came to the light, so obvious that everyone could see them." *"When I saw you in economic ruin, it was not a punishment as you thought, but a blessing,"* the Lord told her. "*Yes, that bankruptcy was to strip you of that god that you served!*"

We must extract the cement we have poured into our souls, the steel with which we have girded our souls, the cage we've built around ourselves. We may have to cast it out by name ("spirit of indifference," "spirit of hardness").

Each day is the first day of the rest of your life and the opportunity for a new start.

Daily, your blackboard can be wiped clean.

Evil will leave as you pray, as you sacrifice, as you suffer, as you name it, as you partake of the sacraments, as you expiate; mainly, as you love. God presents opportunities all day every day. Seize each. Halt darkness in its tracks. Watch each moment. If darkness is already there, expel it. For over the course of life, there is *accumulation*. There are curses. One sin expands into another. There are family curses. There is a proliferation. If we allow a temptation to repeat itself—to traverse past the threshold of thought (if we take it to our imaginations, and then find evil delight in repeating it)—a door opens. Other things enter. The soul is breached. Temptations grow addictive. We enjoy the tang of wrong thoughts, believing they're harmless as long as we don't act on them. We justify dislike, lust, criticism.

All these things we bring with us if they're not purged from the depths of our souls along with the hardness and stones in our hearts—breaking faults that may have come to us down through the ages; as Thomas á Kempis (in *Imitation of Christ*) noted, "So long as we live in this world we cannot escape suffering and temptation. Whence it is written in Job: 'The life of man upon earth is a warfare.'"

"Many special spirits at this time on the earth are here to break traditions of ancestors," said a near-death researcher named Sarah Hinze. "Great traditions that are harsh and disturbing to life, that may cause sadness and pain, such as addictions: Many of us are here to break those chains."

Everyone must watch and guard in prayer lest the devil who never sleeps finds occasion to deceive. Minus humility and love, we have little chance. It doesn't matter what we think (*"I'm tired of all this love stuff . . ."*). It matters what God thinks. (Virtually no account of the afterlife fails to mention love as of paramount importance.)

Simple fact.

We ignore this at our peril.

We can all correct it.

Start by "feeling" your heart.

Is it soft enough?

Can it grieve quickly for a person weeping on TV?

Is it malleable?

Does it contain stones?

We may call it hardness of heart or specks in the eyes.

Both accumulate. Both cause "unfeeling." Both cause blindness. To be poorly sighted is to be in the dark. After a life of immorality and abortion and unbelief, Polo said she found herself in a place of tunnels and "roamed in those tunnels, in the frightening darkness, until I arrived to an obscurity that cannot be compared to anything else. I can only say that a comparison would be the darkest corner on earth compared to the full sunlight at midday. Down there, the darkness generates pain, horror, and shame. It smells terribly. It is a living obscurity, yes, it is alive: there the mind is dead or inert. At the end of my descent, running along those tunnels, I arrived at a level place. I was frantic; I wanted to get out of there with all my strength: it was the same will that I had used to progress in life, but now it did not help me at all, because there I was and there I remained. At a certain point, I saw the ground open up like a great mouth. It was enormous and alive. Alive! I felt my body empty in a startling way, and under me an incredible frightening abyss opened. It was horrible, but what chilled me the most was that there you could not feel the Love of God even a little; there was not even a little drop of hope."

Her greed, her immorality, and her indifference—her resentment—were now her very surroundings.

You make the choice. You create what will be around you. Free will and knowledge go with you. You fashion your eternity.

Ego binds one to the earth.

We must adopt the Sacred Heart of Divine Mercy.

We must be clean and pure like the Immaculate mother who watches us and wants to help.

The "exterior" is what we are on earth; the interior is the light of infinity.

Purgatory is for those who need the exterior burned off.

We choose light or darkness here and thereafter.

Sister Lucia of Fatima said that "hell is a reality, continue to preach about hell, for Our Lord Himself spoke of hell and it is in the Holy Scriptures. God condemns no one to hell. People condemn themselves to hell. God has given mankind the freedom of choice, and He respects this human freedom."

The same message has come from the reputed site of Medjugorje. In greatest danger, it is indicated, are atheists, "those who do not know the Love of God," in the words of a visionary there.

"We saw many people in hell," said another seer named Vicka Ivankovic Mijatovic. "Many are there already, and many more will go there when they die . . . The Blessed Mother says that those people who are in hell are there because they chose to go there. They wanted to go to hell . . . We all know that there are persons on this earth who simply don't admit that God exists, even though He helps them, gives them life and sun and rain and food. He always tries to nudge them onto the path of holiness. They just say they don't believe, and they deny Him. They deny Him, even when it is time to die. And they continue to deny Him, after they are dead. It is their choice. It is their will that they go to hell. They choose hell."

There is fire or dark (or both).

In Moscow an atheist psychologist named Dr. George Rodonaia who was "killed" by a car in 1976 said: "The first thing I remember about my near death experience is that I discovered myself in a realm of total darkness. I had no physical pain; I was still somehow aware of my existence as George, and all about me there was darkness, utter and complete darkness—the greatest darkness ever, darker than any dark, blacker than any black. This was what surrounded me and pressed upon me. I was horrified! I wasn't prepared for this at all. I was shocked to find that I still existed, but I didn't know where I was. The one thought that kept rolling through my mind was, 'How can I be when I'm not?'"

Chapter 13

There are "doors" before the tunnel and the devil is at a number of them, trying to entice us to a place of darkness that we would then struggle, desperately, to climb out of—where we would find no exit.

"Satan is the master of illusion," writes a Seattle woman named Betty. "[The devil] mirrors life, creating false images that deceive even the most astute. He cleverly counterfeits true principles and holds false ones up for admiration. Fortunately, a false spirit posing as an angel of light casts a long, dark shadow. That is the nature of evil. It is a tree that bears bitter fruit that can always be detected over time. Evil will take on any form necessary to tempt us, to claim us, hoping we don't look too closely at its real composition. Remember, like cleaves to like. A darkened soul is more apt to receive a shadowy visitor. Various doors stand before us each day, and we choose which ones to enter. Satan uses negative energies to deceive us into choosing doors which lead into his world."

He makes us tired. He makes us too "busy." He preoccupies us. He inserts thoughts even into our sleep. He nudges us into arguments. Fortunately, we have the ultimate protection of Jesus, and special added protection through the Blessed Mother, through the gifts of the Church.

"The most important thing I know, I guess, is to remember to constantly be looking skyward and not to be deceived by the binding ability earth has on us in the form of our egos," said another witness to the afterlife. "Weeks after my experience, my feet didn't touch the ground. I was so incredibly happy. I was loving with everyone that I had contact with because *I could see through their problems* and often know just the right thing to say to get them to a higher place. It was amazing. I felt as if I was acting out Heaven on earth."

Contrast hell with Heaven:

"The streets were all very broad and smooth and paved with marble and precious stones of every kind," said Rebecca Springer of paradise. "Though they were thronged with people intent on various duties, not a speck of debris or even dust was visible anywhere. Was there night there? Empathically, no! What, for want of a better word, we call *day* was full of glorious radiance, a roseate golden light which was everywhere. There is no language known to mortals that can describe this marvelous glory. It flooded the sky; it was caught up and reflected in the waters; it filled all Heaven with joy and all hearts with song. After a period much longer than our earthly day, this glory mellowed and softened until it became a glowing light full of peace. But there was no darkness, no dusky shadows even—only a restful softening of glory. No fear of harm or danger! No dread of ill or anxiety that a mishap might occur! Security! Security and joy and peace! The material out of which my robe was fashioned was unlike anything I had ever seen. It was soft and light and shone with a faint luster, reminding me more of silk crepe than anything I could recall, only infinitely more beautiful. It fell about me in soft, graceful folds, which the water seemed to have rendered even more lustrous. Before us spread a lake as smooth as glass, but flooded with a golden glory caught from the heavens. It was like a sea of molten gold. Far, far away, across its shining waters, arose the domes and spires of what seemed to be a mighty city. A sacredness enfolds it, and curious eyes should not look upon it. Suffice it to say that no joy we know on earth, however rare, however sacred, can be more than the faintest shadow of the joy we find there."

Noted another named Boris Pilipshuk, "When I entered into the city through the gates, I stood in admiration. The city was made completely of gold. The gold was so pure—I had never seen such brilliance before. Gold streets, houses of gold, gold doors—everything was made of gold, transparent like glass." (See *Revelation* 21:18: "And the street of the city was pure gold, as it were, transparent glass.")

"I recall standing up and pushing the blades of grass to the side, revealing a river right in front of me, running from my right to my left, and I was amazed that I could see right to the bottom of this beautiful river," said a man named Jim Wilhelm. "The river was very deep. I was amazed at how clearly I could see the bright shiny stones at the river's bottom. They looked like clear, shiny jewels. Never had I ever felt this happy, and music was everywhere, and it sounded so beautiful it defies description."

"The main message I brought back," said Dr. Rodonaia, "is that love is what cannot be changed. It is everlasting. And love is with life always, together. Love is an eternity. Love is a basic of humankind. Love is what keeps this earth alive. We are alive because of love. Darkness is the separation from light, from love, from God."

Besteman described "hundreds of rainbows" pouring out of a door. If a blade of grass was pulled out, it replanted itself. If fruit was picked, a replacement grew. If a leaf dropped, it reattached.

In Heaven, we are not subject to decay. We are unique for eternity. We have continuity with "who we were" but—as we by now know so well—are vastly changed.

The new "body" is perfect.

Isn't the Virgin also described in like fashion—swathed in self-luminous, radiant, mysterious colors?

Earth is a photographic negative of that world.

While most appear young and at their prime without the physical faults they bore on earth a spirit can appear in whichever way best suits a situation, dressed for example as a janitor if that's how a relative entering Heaven would best recognize him.

We bring identity.

"When we die our attitudes, demeanor, and personality remain with us," says a woman who should know.

We are with relatives just as Scripture says: "Go, tell my servant David, 'When your time comes and you rest with your ancestors, I will raise up your heir after you . . . and I will make his kingdom firm'" (*2 Samuel* 7).

Nothing dies. Nothing injures. You breathe waters. You drink light. They purge. They heal. There is no loneliness whatsoever.

When we're not prepared for the transition, however, there can be consternation. We could get "stuck" in that tunnel (or here on earth, or halfway). This may happen through fear, disbelief, over-attachment, lack of faith, or lack of knowledge. With Christ we have a sure way.

I know a case where a man who had recently died was spotted on a corner where he seemed to be looking at a book, then upward, then to the book again, as if trying to figure his way "up"—just standing there, as if to ponder his new and apparently befuddling circumstance. (He vanished when the driver who saw him looked back in the mirror.)

Such spirits surround us. It seems they are there before the tunnel, or sometimes in it—not sure how to make the transition. "I can remember faces in the blackness calling out to me; inviting me to join their wall," said a woman named Rebecca. "I think that the people I saw were those who are not ready to cross over just yet and they are the ones that are seen as ghosts. Anyway I was drawn towards them until a light came flying towards me, it was a bird; the bird symbol of peace, to be exact. Its light guided me towards an even brighter light that felt welcoming. When the brightness cleared I could see a line of steps with angels on either side singing some song I could not make out. It didn't take me long to climb the stairs despite the fact that they seemed to go on forever."

Dr. George Ritchie recalled that as the Lord was showing him earthbound spirits, "the Light [of Jesus] drew me inside a dingy bar and grill near what looked like a large naval base. A crowd of people, many of them sailors, lined the bar three deep, while others jammed wooden booths along the wall. Though a few were drinking beer, most of them seemed to be belting whiskies as fast as the two perspiring bartenders could pour them. Then I noticed a striking thing. A number of the men standing at the bar seemed unable to lift their drinks to their lips. Over and over I watched them clutch at their shot glasses, hands passing through the solid tumblers, through the heavy wooden counter top, through the very arms and bodies of the drinkers around them. It was obvious that the living people, the ones actually drinking, talking, jostling each other, could neither see the desperately thirsty disembodied beings among them, nor feel their frantic pushing to get at those glasses." (When sailors passed out, claimed Ritchie, the deceased would attempt to enter them in order to re-experience alcohol, which is what bound them to earth. It gives new meaning to the nickname for liquor: "spirits")!

Noted Dr. Ritchie, "An eternity like that—the thought sent a chill shuddering through me—surely that would be a form of hell. I had always thought of hell, when I thought of it at all, as a fiery place somewhere beneath the earth where evil men like Hitler would burn forever.

"But what if one level of hell existed right here on the surface—unseen and unsuspected by the living people occupying the same space.

"What if it meant remaining on earth but never again able to make contact with it?

"To want most, to burn with most desire, where you were most powerless—that would be hell indeed."

Ritchie also had seen a large flat terrain with spirits of the deceased trying to battle each other. "Although they appeared to be literally on top of each other, it was as though each man was boxing the air," he wrote. "At last I realized that of course, having no substance, they could not actually touch one another. They could not kill, though they clearly wanted to, because their intended victims were already dead, and so they hurled themselves at each other in a frenzy of important rage. If I suspected before that I was seeing hell, now I was sure of it. Up to this moment the misery I had watched consisted in being chained to a physical world of which we were no longer part. Now I saw that there were other kinds of chains. Here were no solid objects or people to enthrall the soul. These creatures seemed locked into habits of mind and emotion, into hatred, lust, destructive thought-patterns. Even more hideous than the bites and kicks they exchanged, were the sexual abuses they were performing in feverish pantomime. It was impossible to tell if the howls of frustration which reached us were actual sounds or only the transference of despairing thoughts. Indeed in this disembodied world it didn't seem to matter. Whatever anyone thought, however fleetingly or unwillingly, was instantly apparent to all around him, more completely than words could have expressed it, faster than sound waves could have carried it. And the thoughts most frequently communicated had to do with the superior knowledge, or abilities, or background of the thinker. 'I told you so!' 'I always knew!' 'Didn't I warn you!' were shrieked into the echoing air over and over. With a feeling of sick familiarity I recognized here my own thinking. This was me, my very tone of voice—the righteous one, the award-winner, the churchgoer."

Do not carry "destructive thought-patterns" to the threshold.

Go through your life and each day take a different phase of it, asking the Holy Spirit, through Jesus, with Mary, and especially at Communion, to wash away all that could cause a scene like the one Dr. Ritchie says he saw or anything near it.

We want to be "chain-breakers," not the chained.

Ask the Lord to lead you on expiating "categories" of darkness such as drugs, the occult, pornography, fornication, or whatever else might be in your past. You will find that some of the categories are actually part of the same package (for example, pornography and fornication).

When we die the exterior is stripped from us. We will be in a place surrounded by those who are most like us. We take our essence.

There are many levels.

Pray for everyone, everyday—even those who honk at you—and your destiny will be pleasant.

Act with love and purity of intention.

Let your first impression of others be that they are good.

Patience is a virtue; lack of patience is a sin.

Let nothing be an affront.

Don't let the devil trick you into thinking his thoughts are yours.

"Our spirits grow strong," said Betty, "through adversity."

There is what they call the "law of the garbage truck."

A man once related how his taxi driver smiled, waved to, and blessed everyone who acted rudely to him. This must have been a city like New York. The driver knew that the reason most folks lash out is because they're frustrated (or fearful: this is a main motive in anger), and bear "garbage" inside.

Stuff had been heaped upon them.

They're seeking an outlet.

They found you.

This is an opportunity.

The answer is to take their garbage: be nice to those who are not nice to you, blessing people who curse you! Jesus told us to do this. Feel joy in serving in such a way.

Don't mind being on the receiving end.

It won't stick.

Just make sure the trash doesn't come from *you* (in which case stick it does).

Hover on wrong emotions and you energize them.

When one falls, it affects the entirety.

Knowing this, how could we root against, denounce, or scoff at a soul: why would we neglect to pray for the downtrodden, even the vilest of criminals, knowing of this connection?

Each person is an entity of equal value placed where he or she is to learn from that experience.

On the other side, the cleaning woman may be of higher authority than the billionaire who owns the skyscraper, the hotel, the mall she cleans.

These too are among those surprises I have mentioned: there are great people, deeply spiritual people, in all walks and stations of life (including, perhaps, the billionaire). What if it's the case that the beggar on the corner is going through that experience in order to learn humility? It's what we have shed when life is over and what we have learned that counts. Knowledge, we take with us. Our caring is in our account. All spiritual progress, big or "small," is important. Remember always that we're spiritual beings having a physical experience. Our spiritual nature is who we really are.

Up there at the gate, the Lord removes what is not your fault.

You don't bring embarrassment.

How could you be embarrassed in a place where everyone not only knows but *understands* everything about you?

You don't take loneliness. (How could you be lonely in a place where there are throngs of relatives?) You don't bring depression. (It would be impossible to be depressed in a place of such light.) You don't bring fright. (In Heaven, and even purgatory, the devil can no longer reach you.) You don't bring worry because now you know there's nothing whatsoever to fret *about*. There is no apprehension of dying for the obvious reason that there is no longer death. This we will finally see for ourselves!

When we endure we transcend.

As a man named Alex Hermosillo of Tempe, Arizona, recounted after he "flat-lined":

"I began to fly through the clouds, moving fast, broke through the clouds, going to a destination quickly and all of my fear, shame, and grief that I had experienced on earth was just pulled right out of me. It was the most joyous time of my entire life," he said, as he encountered many people he knew in this place where the soul now "emanates light."

"Each one had a different amount of light, some had so much light it was like looking into the sun; others had very little light, but were right there," he said. "The light was a reflection of who they were on earth, so if an individual was judgmental, hateful, had vanity and ego, they had a little bit of light. Those who were kind, loving, helped others in their community, just good souls, they were shining brighter."

"A high spiritual being had graded me and there were two other spiritual beings, one on my right," recalls G. Gordon Allen, a formerly wealthy financial adviser from Seattle who succumbed in 1993 (and radically altered his life after). "The thought was communicated to me that all the skills and all the talents that I had been given were for a purpose greater than what I had used them for, that there had been another purpose and they should now be applied to that purpose. That's the moment my life changed." "I was just so focused on my career that I was letting what's really important fall by the wayside," said a lawyer who had the same experience. "God loves you more than you've ever known and knows your circumstances, what you're going through. I used to wake up with a knot in my stomach. I wake up now with joy in my heart. I understand now what's really important."

Anything that diminishes love will be a burden.

It goes to this word: selfishness.

We don't want to leave this life with selfish ambition.

"How many have engaged themselves hour after hour for the world when they could have easily abbreviated such contacts," stated the 1931 missive. "How many hours they could have saved for internal prayer and silent visits to the tabernacle. How many such precious hours were jested away and thus lost for God and for eternity. How many minutes they could have saved our Eucharistic Savior, if the soul had had a true hunger to perform its duties for the love of God alone."

Chapter 14

Do everything with "purity of intention" and you will achieve elevated vision.

It's important.

This is spiritual eyesight.

It is when we see above petty antagonisms.

(It's when we can even *enjoy* the challenge of animosity!)

With every adversity that causes us to advance we overcome oppression.

Earth is a place of adversity. It is to develop our spiritual "muscles." Each time we transcend a difficulty we are stronger.

Nothing purifies more than sending love to those who attack you. "How often virtues are stained and sullied, when they come from the natural, when they are not in the Grace of God, when they are tainted by selfish motive or a lack of humility, while they are untainted—stainless—when they come from a heart blazing with love," says the revelation from 1931. See opponents as *opportunities*. Grow muscle through resistance. Speak maturity into your soul. A "fiery dart" can not penetrate the bubble of humility.

It bounces off. Anger also. (Remember that rage is often caused by fear and perfect love thus casts this out also.)

In this way we progress toward our missions.

I'd like to take a moment to discuss this further: the job that God has set before us to do. "You have things to do." "You're not ready yet." "God has a job for you." "The Lord wants you to finish." So many times after a narrow escape from death souls come back not just because of a doctor's skill, not due to good "luck," not through sheer human will, but because God has ordained it. He wants something else. The job is not complete. The person is not ready.

This job—our missions—is often indicated to us through "signs."

Follow the roadway of your *higher* passions.

Analyze your challenges.

Analyze your pains.

Notice where you find frustration and where you find victory.

As a preacher said, find your role in what "compels and excites you, compels you to diligence, to hard work, yet work done with joy, noticing those things you do that you're passionate about, that spark your creativity, those things that you get energy from when you do them and you find fulfillment in doing, not in getting paid for it but simply in doing it. Those things that we do that put us in that kind of environment are our natural, most organic habitat that make us most effective in our careers, entrepreneurial pursuits, our friendships, and lives. So many people don't do that. We spend so much time doing what we have to do and not enough time doing what we were created to do."

There are large signs. But there are also little ones. They're found in the natural course of life: Many times we are going too fast to spot them. We race right past God's communication. There's too much noise to hear Him. We're too busy to see our course; we're too busy to help someone old; we're too preoccupied to read with our children, to help someone elderly, maybe just to call somebody—when in fact doing so is far more important to God than the "big" things we are in such a hurry to accomplish, which are often based in pride.

It is through the portal of your heart that you enter eternity.

If we could slow time, if it *were* like eternity, where there's no past, present, or future, just *now*, we'd be able to see the "great" in what seems "minor," the big in what seems so small, the worth of what seems worthless. Signs come in many forms: in the way we feel, in what we read, in what we hear from the mouths of others, through ailments, through what makes us feel healthy, through what we need, through defeat, through victory, just as—through a cough or sneeze—we sense a cold; signs come through who attracts us and who is antagonistic, through comradery and "enemies," through coincidence, through success, through failure, through dreams. (Saint Joseph was warned in this manner!) In signs we may be led to a vital purpose. Look to discover your mission in the pains, victories, and challenges of your life. *What was set before you? How did you respond?* Your reaction to challenges will inform you of how you have handled your purpose as well as what it is—and of what direction to take. Your purpose goes to who you really are, so it is critical. "Yet I consider life of no importance to me, if only I may finish *my course* and the ministry that I received from the Lord Jesus, to bear witness to the Gospel of God's Grace," wrote Saint Paul (*Acts* 20; my italics).

When what you are doing is something for the Glory of God—whatever it is—it's part of your master plan (unless it comes from the part of you that wants to flaunt).

What seems worthwhile? What causes you to feel content? What brings peace? What leads you to joy—big marker that one? Is there spiritual baggage? Does it bind you, hold you back?

Your mission is reached on the road to your destiny. "Now my fear is not dying," said a near-deather named Nathan. "My fear is not living and doing the things I was born to do; if you have a passion or a yearning to do something, you need to do it"—as long as it does not originate in your ego (I want to be a movie star; I want to be an author; I want to be a CEO; I want the Pope to know who I am).

That old expression "go with the flow" has special meaning when the flow is the Holy Spirit, when it is in flux with the "living waters," when you find your "original splendor." How often do we lament that God "did not answer" our prayers, complaining that faith doesn't seem to be working because we didn't get this or didn't get that or because something did not happen as *we* wanted it to happen?

These are signs that what we are seeking may not be in accordance with His Plan and may originate in pride. Isn't God the author of subtlety? Isn't coincidence His way of remaining anonymous? And when we're doing right, doesn't it almost seem like you can feel Him smile? But, too, if we trip over a crack, it may be a sign that we need to fix the sidewalk (or avoid it). If a branch is drooping on a tree, the tree could have insects. One must investigate. There is discernment. A *tick-tick* in the motor may indicate car trouble down the road.

(Are there tick-ticks in your life?)

God repeats and so if we keep hearing about a person, or a place, or a thing, maybe there is something there for us. If we keep running into someone, perhaps we have something we need to do with or for them. (If we keep reading about vitamins, maybe we need to eat more spinach!)

There are big signs. There are signs in nature. There are signs in the life spans of leaves, in the spot where the sun rises, in the first seedlings that whisper of spring, in the clouds, gathering, shifting, that portend a shower; in the sway of the wind.

There are miraculous signs: There are the roses that appear after a novena to the Little Flower; there is the scent of sanctity around mystics.

When these come—when your intuition is alerted—pay heed. Strike a balance between seeing too much into signs ("confirmations") and not noting them enough; always seek the "harmony" of life, whereby each occurrence sings to another.

Signs can come when we stumble, when we feel too much resistance, when it seems like we're forcing things, when what we seek creates tension, when the fruit is insomnia, when there is confusion (a mark of evil)—just as our bodies tell us what is good and not so good when what we eat causes acid reflux or allergies (as there are also "spiritual allergies" and "spiritual indigestion"); when we don't heed the sign of small pains, we risk encountering larger ones.

A sign can come when something or someone makes you feel like someone or something you are not. On the other hand, when we're on the path to our destinies, it feels like we're headed home (because we are).

The signs of your mission come by way of what you love doing, what makes you feel comfortable, what makes you feel holiest, what you have energy for, what brings satisfaction, what is hard but joyous, what fits like an old shoe, what's done with no selfishness, what requires work but not tension, what serves others, what feels good even when exhausting, what fits your personality, what allows for pure motive, what brings you closest to God.

So many seek to be "big" in the eyes of the world, when what God often sees is greatness in what is small, in personal contact, in unworldliness.

"Being successful and fulfilling your life's purpose are not at all the same thing," notes author Rick Warren. *"You can reach all your personal goals, become a raving success by the worlds standard, and still miss your purpose in this life."*

This is a "secret of eternity."

And if there is greatness in what is little, there are signs there, in everyday life, also. When something causes us peace and joy and energy or, on the other hand, trepidation, depression, weightiness, or outright fear—when we feel the bottom of our stomachs fall—these too are signs of our times. It doesn't have to be a hurricane. You don't need an aurora borealis! Throughout this journey called life are sign-posts. Some are big—billboards. Most: small. Some: microscopic. All are noticed (illumined) in a state of prayer: *"Lord, illumine the little things in my life."*

While on earth, we define ourselves by our physical bodies, because it's the "us" we see, but a frame of mind focused on the body and its interaction with mere physical objects and other "bodies" (as opposed to seeing them as souls) stifles us and can compromise the mission God has designed.

Remember too that the body is just your "spacesuit" during this journey on planet earth. It's the first thing—the body—we leave!

It's funny how those who died say they suddenly saw their bodies as familiar but not the real "them," and didn't want to re-enter them anymore than put on a dirty pair of socks.

As Scripture says, we're given a glorified body, a spiritual one (*Philippians* 3:20-21).

"I started to float back to earth, and the closer I got the dirtier and uglier it appeared," said a woman who lived in California at the time of her experience (which occurred during the crash of a motorcycle). "I then felt myself enter into my body on the operating table with a sound like *whoosh*!"

"I was twenty-nine years old and had gone to the dentist's office," related Dr. Lani Leary. "They were using 'laughing gas' at the time. I think my body just said, 'What is this?' and I went into shock. One minute I was in the dentist's chair and the next I was up at the ceiling looking down at this body. As I looked at my twenty-nine-year-old body I felt as if it were just a piece of clothing. I had a fondness for it, I knew it, I had used it well, but it was time to go to the Salvation Army. I didn't feel connected to it. I felt no fear, no pain, no anxiety. The dentist was freaking out and I was trying to tell him from up there that it was okay, but he didn't get it. I had no sense of time. *There was no anxiety, no sense of passing time.* I don't know how long I was up there in the corner. The next thing I knew it was as if I had turned around and was going into a tunnel. And my mother, who had been dead for fifteen years, was right at the tunnel. I can still see it. She was beautiful and whole and vibrant, and she did not die that way. She was healed. Her arms were outstretched to me. We communicated telepathically: I thought (a thought), and she received, and she thought, and I heard. My ego was not present. My ego would have wanted me to stay with my mother for years and years and years and tell her every single first date I had and my wedding and about my child, but my ego was not present because I knew from a soul level at that moment that she had always been with me. We had never been apart." Lani entered the Great Light and felt she and the Light were made of the same substance—"bliss doesn't come close to the word"; she felt completely at home. "I knew I was forgiven for everything I thought was unforgiveable," she remarked, adding, as the vast majority do, that she didn't want to return to her physical self. She was in a place with "love beyond all measure" but heard the Voice from the Light say, *"You must go back,"* and when she objected It said, *"You have work to do. You must go back."*

Chapter 15

Once on the other side, you are *there*.

There are no more threats.

There is no imperfection.

Doubt vanishes.

Not an ounce remains.

The more faith, the higher the place.

You'll bring no sadness, no maladies, with you.

If it sounds too good to be true, it's too good (considering God's absolute goodness) not to be.

On the other side, those who were ill, who were missing limbs, who were hunched over in life, who had been unsightly, wore frayed clothes, had blemishes, or the worst tumors, the worst possible ailments, unto amputation, ebola, leprosy, suddenly find themselves—in completely perfect health. We don't take any dis-ease (which originally meant "lack of peace") with us—not to Heaven. We have no wear and tear with us. We don't bring old age. There is a popular painting showing a crippled elderly woman entering a looking glass between here and there and being greeted as a young woman on the other side by Jesus.

There's truth there. Old out; new in.

There is the overwhelming atmosphere of well-being.

No one is obese; none is emaciated; no one bears scars. Most look like they're in their twenties or early thirties. Apparently, that's the popular age to choose. Historically, the Blessed Mother is described as young, radiating, sometimes even in her teens, "a woman clothed with the sun," the sun being the closest a metaphor for the brilliant light that stands as the single most immediate depiction of Heaven, that doesn't, however, afflict the eyes, doesn't blind, doesn't burn even though it is of greater intensity—infinitely—than what is in the sky here on earth. There is light all around. Everywhere. No shadows. All-pervasive. It comes from God. It contains the universe. Prophets in the Bible called it "glory." We encounter it upon release. We must never hold onto darkness. Sometimes, we do so out of insecurity. We must release insecurity, along with suffering. All will be illumined. A woman from Singapore named Anita Moorjani said: "If you imagine you are in a warehouse that is completely dark and you have one little flashlight and that's the only light you have to navigate through this warehouse, and you're shining the light to navigate through this warehouse and you're shining your path ahead of you, so you're not bumping into anything: Imagine if the lights go on—huge floodlights—and this whole warehouse just [suddenly] lights up, and you realize it's *much* larger than you ever imagined. When all the lights are on you can see everything at once. The warehouse is lined with shelves and shelves, of all kinds, of different things, different colors, different shapes. Suddenly you understand that when you just had the flashlight, you could only see one thing at a time, but now you can see everything all at once and they all exist simultaneously. For the first time in my entire life did I feel I was loved and accepted unconditionally for who I am. I felt like I was connected to everyone and everything."

"It was mind-blowing and breathtaking," said another seer. "The most beautiful thing that ever happened." "A vast space, and it has a brilliant light which does not leave it," says one more seer. "It is a life which we do not know here on earth. We saw people dressed in gray, pink, and yellow robes. They were walking, praying, and singing. Small angels were flying above them. They were in small groups. The Blessed Mother showed us how happy these people are. It is impossible to describe with words the great happiness I saw in Heaven."

There is not the "gray" of our world. It is something *like* gray, but not gray; *like* yellow, but not yellow. The people this visionary saw were communicating with the Blessed Mother in something she described as "like a tunnel, only it wasn't exactly like a tunnel, but a tunnel is the closest comparison. People in Heaven know the absolute fullness of a created being."

The absolute fullness of a created being.

Like everyone in existence is embracing you.

"If I thought of Heaven too much—I would die of loneliness," said a young boy who likewise saw the Blessed Mother.

When the financier from Seattle had his near-death brush—going in and out of our reality, during a bout with congestive heart failure—at one point he encountered a totally gorgeous woman who upon seeing him was excited and full of joy. Though Protestant, he believes that was the Virgin Mary, bedecked in blue. Afterward, as he regained consciousness, he noted nurses swarming around—coming in and out—and was told it wasn't just because of his close call but to see a mysterious soft blue light—sublime, lambent—that remained there for half an hour on the wall behind him.

A radiance, a robe, a smile that sparkles.

This is the attire of Heaven.

Purgatory is quite different.

It is a place, one of the seers said, that's "foggy, it is ash gray. It is misty. You cannot see people there. It is as if they are immersed in deep clouds. You can feel that the people in the mist are traveling, hitting each other. They can pray for us but not for themselves. They are desperately in need of our prayers. The Blessed Mother asks us to pray for the poor souls in purgatory, because during their life here, one moment they thought there was no God; then they recognized Him; then they went to purgatory where they saw there is a God, and now they need our prayers. With our prayers we can send them to Heaven. The biggest suffering that souls in purgatory have is that they see there is a God, but they did not accept Him here on earth. Now they long so much to come close to God. Now they suffer so intensely, because they recognize how much they have hurt God, how many chances they had on earth, and how many times they disregarded God."

"In Purgatory there are different levels," said the Blessed Mother in former Yugoslavia. "The lowest is close to hell and the highest gradually draws near Heaven. The majority of people go to purgatory. Many go to hell. A small number go directly to Heaven."

To be in the "small number": belief is crucial. We take faith, for sure. We are wrapped in it! We also, though, can take with us rejection of God. Absolute such *rejection* leads to a place of His absolute *absence*, which means hell. A seer said it is a "self-chosen" suffering that is "beyond your ability to comprehend."

Those headed for hell know it but—astoundingly, in many cases—don't seem to care.

They sense it.

They realize how dangerous it is to dismiss God.

Yet, in their blind pride they have grown irrational.

I heard seers speak of viewing a beautiful young woman entering the fire of hell and turning into an ugly, half-human, half-animal entity (the classical description of a demon). "When they came out, they were raging and smashing everything around and hissing and gnashing and screeching," said the second visionary I mentioned.

Drugs also seem to lead many to hell, or deep purgatory, perhaps what Scripture calls the "outer darkness" (if this Scripture does not mean hell). There can be an extreme cold (something *like* cold, in the way of the "spiritual flesh") or fire. Jesus warned of a darkness where there'd be "weeping and gnashing of teeth" (*Matthew* 8:12).

The question is whether that refers to deep purgatory (since there is weeping, as opposed to rage) or hell.

Perhaps it's an element of both states.

This is what eternity is: a state of being. Our "state of being" fashions itself around us (and those in a similar state). Upon the great transition we find ourselves surrounded by those who are like of mind and heart; who have the same level of faith and love; who are as kind (or unkind) as we are. There's no drastic change in personality. You take who you are and in many ways find yourself in the same state of mind, at the same level, as you ended up with on earth.

There may be countless levels. Since the beginning of time, scientists tell us, there have been dozens of billions of humans. Every time one of those billions goes to a place of suffering, we all lose. A person in hell is a defeat for all of us! Yet, free will prevails. Those in a dismal "in-between" zone are those who were filled with doubt, who prayed and believed only occasionally, not certain God existed, who transgressed freely, forgetting love.

The more such folks reject Him, the deeper they go.

The deeper they are, the more they rage.

The hotter. The darker. The colder.

Let us not deceive ourselves: there are destinations that are rancid, that are dungeons.

There are many "places"—dimensions of all sorts. Eventually the condemned lose most human resemblance. Their hatred: they carried this with them; they harbored it; they refused to relinquish it. It materialized. To call to God would be to admit they were wrong.

Pride hates.

Humility loves.

These beings hate and seek to drag everyone they can into their "zone." Saint Teresa described the entrance to hell as like "a very long, narrow passage, like a furnace, very low, dark, and closely confined; the ground seemed to be full of water which looked like filthy, evil-smelling mud, and in it were many wicked-looking reptiles. At the end there was a hollow place scooped out of a wall, like a cupboard, and it was here that I found myself in close confinement. But the sight of all this was pleasant by comparison with what I felt there. My feelings could not possibly be exaggerated, nor can anyone understand them. I felt fire within my soul the nature of which I am utterly incapable of describing. My bodily sufferings were so intolerable that, though in my life I have endured the severest sufferings of this kind—the worst it is possible to endure, the doctors say, such as the shrinking of the nerves during my paralysis and many and diverse more, some of them, as I have said, caused by the devil—none of them is of the smallest account by comparison with what I felt then, to say nothing of the knowledge that they would be endless and never-ceasing. And even these are nothing by comparison with the agony of my soul, an oppression, a suffocation and an affliction so deeply felt, and accompanied by such hopeless and distressing misery, that I cannot too forcibly describe it."

It is the absence of light—the Light of God—that causes the inconceivable, palpable, horrifying blackness. The saint found herself in what seemed like a hole in the wall—so small she could not sit or lie. "There was no light and everything was in the blackest darkness," wrote Teresa. "I don't understand how this can be, but, although there was no light, it was possible to see everything the sight of which can cause affliction." Wondered the saint after her visions, "How could anything give me satisfaction which was driving me to such an awful place?"

In hell, everything is representative of who we are and what we did on earth. It is a place of intense dread; guttural screams; thousands and thousands of the "dungeons." Bodies are ripped apart, said one fellow, then reassembled, then ripped apart again, as those here experience what they afflicted on others in deed or word (but magnified).

The entities from there—from what Saint Teresa called "that pestilential spot"—afflict us even here on earth. Back in a wakeful state, Teresa knew not to fear devils when she had Jesus.

"Indeed, they seem to be afraid of me," she said. "I have acquired an authority over them, bestowed upon me by the Lord of all, so that they are no more trouble to me now than flies. They seem to me such cowards—as soon as they see that anyone despises them, they have no strength left. They are enemies who can make a direct attack only upon those whom they see as giving in to them, or on servants of God whom, for their own greater good, God allows to be tried and tormented. These devils keep us in terror because we make ourselves liable to be terrorized by contracting other attachments—to honors, for example, and to possessions and pleasures. When this happens, they join forces with us—since, by loving and desiring what we ought to hate, we become our own enemies—and they will do us much harm. When [the devil] sees that such a person's understanding is darkened, he gaily assists him to become completely blind; for if he sees anyone blind enough to find comfort in vanities—and such vanities! for the vanities of this world are like children's playthings—[the devil] sees that he is indeed a child, and treats him as one, making bold to wrestle with him, first on some particular occasion and then again and again."

The very things that invite evil to us on earth can also drag us to darkness after.

Distance yourself from that which afflicts you.

Detach from "toxic" relationships.

The greatest shields: love, faith, and humility.

With those, a bubble of protection forms around us.

We puncture that bubble with sin.

We allow entrance.

Christ in His Mercy is *always* there to instantly repair it for us. We must be sincere. We must ask. We must repent with the *intention of correction.* When we confess, it must come from the heart—thus causing us to cleanse. The Seattle financier said that of twenty-six people who had the negative afterlife encounter in one little survey, all cried out to God—to Jesus—and were raised out of what Storm had called the "pipeline to the cesspool of the universe."

Later in his life, Saint Padre Pio of Pietrelcina seemed to soften his theology. "I believe that not a great number of souls go to hell," he is said to have remarked. "God loves us so much. He formed us in His image. God the Son Incarnate died to redeem us. He loves us beyond understanding. And it is my belief that even when we have passed from the consciousness of the world, when we appear to be dead, God, before He judges us, will give us a chance to see and understand what sin really is. And if we understand it properly, how could we fail to repent?"

Yet, fail a significant number do.

In His final Mercy, God rescues those who relinquish atheism, recognize Him, and repent. We can never judge! We can pray. We see how the emptiness of life transfers into forever. We see how darkness is as darkness was. We see how anger turns into—fire. Engulfs. We go where we belong. We go where we are most comfortable—even if it's hell, if we are comfortable only with the notion that God does not exist or with the emotion of hatred toward Him and others; total arrogance. Should we read such accounts and become afraid? Just more devout. Just more determined. More loving. Whenever a person comes to mind, immediately pray for him and your mind will turn positive, less likely to scan their faults. Mercy trumps all. God looks for any amount, even small, of: wisdom, fortitude, knowledge, piety, respect for His Son, with contrition. Knowledge with perspective is wisdom. He does not care about false piety. He looks for a deep bond built of love. There is, as I said, that Light at the end of the passage.

"It is not a radiance which dazzles, but a soft whiteness and an infused radiance which, without wearying the eyes, causes them the greatest delight; nor are they wearied by the brightness they see in seeing this Divine beauty," says a recent account. "So different from any earthly light is the brightness and light now revealed to the eyes that, by comparison with it, the brightness of our sun seems quite dim and we should never want to open our eyes again for the purpose of seeing it. It is as if we were to look at a very clear stream, in a bed of crystals, reflecting the sun's rays, and then to see a very muddy stream, in an earthly bed and overshadowed by clouds.

"It is a light which never gives place to night, and, being always light, is disturbed by nothing."

In Venezuela, where the Blessed Mother has been seen at a spot called Betania, Our Lady was described as wearing this same soft but bright light, so very light-filled, as at Lourdes, Knock, and Fatima.

At sites of apparition and during prayer groups (wherever the Holy Spirit is), there is a taste and a touch of the portal of Heaven.

At Betania I myself saw an extraordinary light radiate from the sun in a beam of luminosity that formed a detailed, perfect silhouette of the Virgin with arms offering grace as in the famous statue of the Miraculous Medal.

"Little children," she said there, "I call you this day to the fullness of life, that you may live with a conscience clear and responsible for your entrusted mission, with the virtues of faith, hope, and charity. I especially recommend to you purity of intention, humility, simplicity, and obedience to the responsibility contracted with the Lord. Promise to stay on the road of innocence. How lovely is the beauty of innocent children, of those who live spontaneously, naturally, without harming or injuring any human being—helping, inviting all to be brothers and sisters, living life by example, in the Love of the Lord, our Father, that He may give us being, His Life."

"Repent and be baptized and you will receive the gift of the Holy Spirit," says *Acts* (2:38).

Chapter 16

All that is indifferent and false is brought with us if we hold onto it (free will) and eliminated by whatever means deemed necessary by God. Our true selves are humble; we are formed in His image. Ask God this: *am I really humble? If not, show me.* We know we are getting to "who we really are" when we develop simplicity.

Simplicity leads to humility and humility vanquishes fear.

Fear attracts demons.

"It acts like a homing beacon for demons," says a former Satanist who is now a devout Catholic. "Next to anger, fear is another powerful emotion that demons have an insatiable desire for. Fear attracts multiple demons, demons that specialize and are experts in their respective fields such as anxiety, worry, suspicion, self-doubt, and depression to name a few. They always band together and come as a cluster to torment some poor soul caught up in the emotion of fear. A constant state of fear is an open invitation for demons to come barging in and set up a command post in your head."

Humility shoos that away. It means acquiescence. It entails obedience. It commands no stage. It means quiet strength. It involves nothing that is "aggressive." It knows no disdain. Vanity is its opposite, showiness its contradiction. Said an ostentatious CEO who suffered a brain abscess, "I remember laying there quietly and very cognitively knowing that I might die and I wanted to know, *'If I die, what would I meet? What would I face? Where would I go?'* I said a simple prayer, in my thoughts. It was sincere and it was deep and it was true of my heart and the prayer was this, 'If there's a God, I would really truly like to know Who you are.'" It was then, he said, that "something supernatural happened to me. I felt like I was either having a vision or an out-of-body experience. I found myself in a place of great darkness, a place completely isolated from the rest of the world, a place that felt without hope. And I had the awareness, as I was in this darkness, that this is where I'm headed, and it scared me, and in that moment I also saw Jesus and I had this feeling of great peace, of hope, and a sense that I had a choice to make."

We all have choices to make every day.

Many encounter angelic, demonic, or deceased entities as they near death. We finally see what has been around us. We want safety against the entities that come from darkness.

Said Saint Boniface, recounting the experience of a monk who'd died and returned: "Angels of such pure splendor bore him up as he came forth from the body that he could not bear to gaze upon them. 'They carried me up,' he said, 'high into the air.' He said also that there was a crowd of evil spirits and a glorious choir of higher angels. And he said that the wretched spirits and the holy angels had a violent dispute concerning the souls that had come forth from their bodies, the demons bringing charges against them and aggravating the burden of their sins, the angels lightening the burden and making excuses for them. He heard all his own sins, which he had committed from his youth on and had failed to confess or had forgotten or had not recognized as sins, crying out against him, each in its own voice, and accusing his grievously. Everything he had done in all the days of his life and had neglected to confess and many which he had not known to be sinful, all these were now shouted at him in terrifying words. In the same way the evil spirits, chiming in with the vices, accusing and bearing witness, naming the very times and places, brought proofs of his evil deeds; and so, with his sins all piled up and reckoned out, those ancient enemies declared him guilty and unquestionably subject to their jurisdiction. 'On the other hand,' he said, 'the poor little virtues which I had displayed unworthily and imperfectly spoke out in my defense. And those angelic spirits in their boundless love defended and supported me, while the virtues, greatly magnified as they were, seemed to me far greater and more excellent than could have ever been practiced in my own strength.'"

Saint Antony the Great had a vision of "certain bitter and certain things" that wished to hinder his passage through the tunnel, the "veil." As it was written, "And he remembered that this is what the Apostle said, 'according to the prince of the power of the air.' For in it the enemy hath power to fight and to attempt to hinder those who pass through. Wherefore most earnestly he exhorted, 'Take up the whole armor of God, that ye may be able to withstand in the evil day,' that the enemy, 'having no evil thing to say against us, may be ashamed.'"

And then there was Saint Diadochos who reminds us that "if we do not confess our involuntary sins as we should, we shall discover an ill-defined fear in ourselves at the hour of our death. We who love the Lord should pray that we may be without fear at that time; for if we are afraid then, we will not be able freely to pass by the rulers of the netherworld. They will have as their advocate to plead against us the fear which our soul experiences because of its own wickedness. But the soul which rejoices in the love of God, at the hour of its departure, is lifted with the angels of peace above all the hosts of darkness. For it is given wings by spiritual love, since it ceaselessly carries within itself the love which 'is the fulfilling of the law' (*Romans* 13:10)."

A Christian named Yong Thang from Myanmar was given a glimpse of hell before heading for paradise. This occurred in 1980. "I knew where I would be going," he said. "I would be in Heaven! Looking at my wife, I took pity on her as she would be alone for the rest of her life. So I prayed to God to take care of her for her entire life. I committed my life in God's hands in the Name of Jesus. After a while, I saw a cluster of dark clouds descending from the sky. (Though there was a roof on top of me, I could actually see the sky through it.) The dark clouds were approaching me. They landed and stopped above my bed about three feet away. At that very moment, my soul left my body. I looked down and saw my body lying beside my wife. It was completely a lifeless corpse! I was well aware that my body had died. Suddenly, I saw large demons coming from all directions. They gathered around my bed and stared at my body. I then looked towards the sky and shouted, 'Angels! Please protect my body immediately.' Thank God that although I had never known how angels looked like, they appeared when I shouted. Five angels came down immediately from heaven to guard my body. At the same time, the demons, which gathered around my body, disappeared instantly I suddenly remembered what was mentioned in the Bible 'Are they not all ministering spirits sent forth to minister to those who will inherit salvation' (*Hebrews* 1:14)."

There are cases in which there is that last, dark struggle.

It's why we say, *"Hail Queen of Mercy, protect us from the enemy, and receive us at the hour of death."*

"Pilot my wretched soul, pure Virgin, and have compassion on it, as it slides under a multitude of offences into the deep of destruction; and at the fearful hour of death snatch me from the accusing demons and from every punishment," is another prayer (from a Midnight Office for Sunday).

Go to Mary. "*Luke* 1:48 states that all generations to come will call her blessed," wrote Lipsky. "In the *Magnificat* Our Lady said that her soul 'magnifies' the Lord. Just like a magnifying glass, to magnify means to enlarge and make something clearer. She wants to help make God and her Son clearer to you and me. She has been given power over the devil by God! God has given her command over the angels to deploy them to people who sincerely ask for her intervention. She sends help whenever help is needed."

With belief in Christ and the assistance of Mary, with the saints, and our angels, along with prayer, we are completely secure in the passage.

Dark spirits can do nothing.

When a priest I knew named Father Stephen Scheier "died" in a head-on crash in 1985, he recalled that "I was before the judgment seat of Our Lord. I did not see Him. There was much said in regards to my life. The only thing that I did when I heard about particular instances was internally say, 'yes, yes—that's true.' There was no rebuttal. At the end of His speaking, God said, *'The sentence that you will have for all eternity is hell.'* I thought internally, 'I know—this is what I deserve.' At that moment, I heard a female voice. The voice said, *'Son, would You please spare his life?'* Our Lord then said, *'Mother—he has been a priest for twelve years for himself and not for Me . . . Let him reap the punishment he deserves.'* At that, I heard her say again in response, *'But Son, if we give to him special graces and strengths, and come to him in ways he is not familiar with, we can see if he bears fruit . . . If he does not, then Your Will be done.'* There was a very short pause. And the Lord said, *'Mother, he's yours.'*"

She is right there with Him.

Her immaculate heart is next to His.

Never should we forget this.

As in so many cases: there is no disputing the truth. Our souls know the truth and are ready to go where they belong.

How do we live so that we feel confident that our soul will "choose" Heaven when we die?

"The most important thing is that we know that God exists, that we believe in God, that we trust God's Love for us, and that we know there is no definite death for us," said Marija Pavlovic-Lunetti of Medjugorje. "That's why we have to thank Him all the time." Hell, she saw, was a "large space with a big sea of fire in the middle." On purgatory, the seer added, in an excellent book called *Queen of the Cosmos*, by Jan Connell: "It is a large place. It is foggy. It is ash gray. It is misty. You cannot see people there. It is as if they are immersed in deep clouds. You can feel that the people in the mist are traveling, hitting each other. They can pray for us but not for themselves. They are desperately in need of our prayers. The Blessed Mother asks us to pray for the poor souls in purgatory, because during their life here, one moment they thought there is a God, and now they need our prayers. With our prayer we can send them to Heaven. The biggest suffering that souls in purgatory have is that they see there is a God, but they did not accept Him here on earth. Now they long so much to come close to God. Now they suffer so intensely, because they recognize how much they have hurt God, how many chances they had on earth, and how many times they disregarded God."

I respect people of every faith that believe in Him, and have considered many non-Catholic accounts—which lend us insight—but Catholicism has within its doors many secrets to protection: the ultimate secrets, in my opinion, and the best way of attaining the highest places, the special places where Mary is so prominent.

"I saw Heaven as if it were a movie," said seer Mirjana Dragicievic-Soldo. "The first thing I noticed was the faces of the people there; they were radiating a type of inner light which showed how immensely happy they were. The trees, the meadows, the sky are totally different than anything we know on the earth. And the light is much more brilliant. Heaven is beautiful beyond any possible comparison with anything I know of on the earth." Asked about their ages, she said, "They were different from what we are like now. Perhaps they were all around thirty-five years of age. They were walking in a beautiful park. They have everything. They need or want nothing. They are totally fulfilled. They were dressed in the types of clothing that Jesus wore. There are different levels of purgatory. The more you pray on earth, the higher your level in purgatory will be. The lowest level is the closest to hell, where the suffering is the most intense. The highest level is closest to Heaven, and there the suffering is the least. What level you are on depends on the state of purity of your soul. The lower the people are in purgatory and the less they are able to pray, the more they suffer. The higher a person is in purgatory and the easier it is for him to pray, the more he enjoys praying, and the less he suffers."

In a classic called *Purgatory Explained*, Father F.X. Schouppe describes the case of an artist who had great skill and an otherwise exemplary life but once had made a painting that did not conform with Christian modesty. Shortly after his death he appeared to a prior at a monastery, wrapped in flames. "Alas," he explained. "It is on account of the immodest picture that I painted some years ago. When I appeared before the tribunal of the Sovereign Judge, a crowd of accusers came to give evidence against me. They declared that they had been excited to improper thoughts and evil desires by a picture, the work of my hand. In consequence of those bad thoughts some were in purgatory, others in hell. The latter cried for vengeance, saying that, having been the cause of their eternal perdition, I deserved, at least, the same punishment. Then the Blessed Virgin and saints whom I had glorified by my pictures took up my defense. They represented to the Judge that the unfortunate painting had been the work of my youth, and of which I had repented; that I had repaired it afterwards by religious objects which had been the sources of edification to souls. In consideration of these and other reasons, the Sovereign Judge declared that, on account of my repentance and good works, I should be exempt from damnation; but at the same time, He condemned me to these flames until the picture should be burned, so that it could no longer scandalize anyone."

It takes holiness for a good afterlife and as another visionary said, "holiness is simply faithfulness to God in good times and bad."

"The Blessed Mother told me that before God made the world, He knew each of His children of the earth and named each one of us."

Study your fears and ask why you are fearful.

Fear often comes from pride, which Saint Augustine said "is the beginning of all sin." Pride of intellect. Pride of authority or superiority. Pride of ambition. Pride of religiosity. Pride of complacency. Pride of anything physical. Fear comes from sin. It is good to be clear of all sin at all times and on the constant lookout for imperfection of any kind. Yet the actual process of dying is mainly described as a great relief. A great number die, arms reaching forward, with a look of peace.

"Many of us have a fear of death, but there is no need for it," wrote a woman from England who claims to see angels. "At the moment of death there is no pain, no discomfort; some people may have pain right up to that last moment, but then there is none. You have no fear or anxiety—you go freely. Death is like birth; I know you might think that's a strange thing to say, but you are being born into a new life. You actually don't 'die.' It's only this physical shell that you leave—like an empty egg shell. When you die, you are not on your own, you are accompanied all the time by angels and those spirits who have gone before you. You won't want to come back."

As one man in hospice told a priest, "Some evil spirits do not want my soul to go with the loving spirits. They want me to stay with them here on earth after I die. They are afraid if I go with God's angels, I may draw them with me into the Light, which they feel is where judgment occurs."

Our love—and humility—render them inert.

Fear can attract them.

It is when we lack spiritual joy that we seek carnal pleasures (said Saint Augustine).

"Our Lady shows us and gives us the grace to surrender because she's Lady Wisdom," said a holy nun I knew. "Surrender is the highest form of wisdom. We go to Our Lady and beg for the grace to surrender to whatever way God is calling us into deeper purification."

"God and His angels will be with you always, so have no fear," said another who experienced the Great Transition (but came back to tell of it).

Fear not pain.

Unless there is need for special expiation, the Lord will free you from pain even if it looks to those still alive that your body is in agony.

A chiropractic doctor named Frank Novasack Jr. from Pittsburgh was said (in a book, *The Miracle of the Illumination of All Consciences*, by Thomas W. Petrisko) to have had a dream in which "I was close to death and a coming judgment, and I sensed I was traveling to the place of judgment. There were others with me. Everyone else was not taking anything with them, but I felt compelled to pack enough clothes for a period. I sensed that I was going to either purgatory or to hell, and I feared that it was possibly hell. Also accompanying me were two men from my past, who I remembered had personal problems in college.

"I soon found myself getting on an elevator with two large suitcases and then going down many floors. The elevator descended many levels and suddenly I realized that I was possibly getting close to hell. I became frightened about where I was going. Finally, I got off the elevator and I walked down a long corridor that resembled an underground airport shuttle. I then went down another series of elevators, and was again scared that I was about to face hell. Finally, I arrived in this big underground conference auditorium that had a large audience of people in it. There was a lot of noise going on. On a stage-like platform, like a judge's bench, there were people speaking who were talking about morality and ethics. Simultaneously, there were also speakers with microphones in the audience, addressing the people at the different, higher levels in front.

"As I watched I realized that it appeared that a judgment of some kind was occurring, and that there was a great level of suffering being experienced by the people in the audience. I noticed the people were suffering mentally upon the realization of the sins that they had committed, more than anything else. I also understood that they were being shown how they had offended God and how this hurt God. I then noticed a young lady, who was maybe in her late twenties in age, being lectured to about her sin. Once again, I felt a keen, almost painful awareness of sin and the mental grief which outweighed any physical suffering over the offenses towards God. The speaker addressed this young lady about her alcoholism and how it had led her into further sin. But she was in denial and yelled back to the speaker that it wasn't that bad and that she didn't feel like she'd done anything wrong. 'I didn't do anything so bad . . . I didn't do anything so bad,' I heard her say. I eventually woke up in a panic, quite shocked by the dream. I was shaken for days after this and still remember it very clearly. From it all I was left with a deep understanding of how our smallest sins offend God and how intense the psychological and emotional component of our 'judgment' will perhaps be. I also felt I was made aware of how this all is related to the *Act of Contrition* that we say during Confession."

Like Father Sheier, the vast majority argue nothing in the face of incontrovertible truth—even desire to go where they belong. Thus, they "choose" it—whether in the way of what they had done during life or in the "judgment." "This marvelous person showed me my life course, which revealed I was without excuse," said B. W. Melvin. "It was then I knew I was being judged and deserved my fate."

"What shall we say of those who are snatched away by a sudden death?" asked Saint Robert Ballarmine (in *The Art of Dying Well*). "What of those who are afflicted with madness or fall into delirium before Confession? What of those who, being grievously afflicted by their disease, cannot even think of their sins? What of those who sin while dying, or die in sin, as they do who engage in an unjust war or in a duel, or are killed in the act of adultery?

"Prudently to avoid these and other like misfortunes, nothing can be imagined more useful than for those who value their salvation to examine their consciences diligently twice every day, morning and night: what they have done during the night or the preceding day; what they have said, desired, or thought of, into which sin may have entered. And if they discover any mortal sin, let them not defer seeking the remedy of true contrition, but resolve to approach the sacrament of Penance at the very first opportunity. Wherefore, let them ask of God the gift of contrition; let them ponder on the enormity of sin; let them detest their sins from the heart, and seriously ask themselves who is offended and who the offender.

"If this examination is continued morning and night, or at least once a day, it can scarcely happen that we shall die in sin, or mad, or delirious. Thus it will be that, every preparation being made for a good death, its uncertainty will not trouble us, nor will the happiness of eternal life fail us."

"Little" acts of love are crucial.

"What was not important [in the judgment of my life review] was anything that I had owned or known intellectually—there is a sense of intellectual pride—but what was important was the purity and motivation of every action and I recall the most important of my actions, in an instant I would never have recalled, was many years ago when I had worked every summer as a volunteer with retarded children and there was a child one time and I had taken a child aside on a very hot day, not a particularly charming or lovable child, but I wanted this child to feel the love of God that brought him into existence and I took him aside and I just wanted him to feel love and I gave him something to drink," remarked a woman named Reinee. "That was the greatest of all actions and that just filled me with unspeakable, incomprehensible joy. It was not an action I even remembered and one that was not done with any thought of reward. It was motivated by selfless love."

Chapter 17

We get back to who we really are when we love *for real* and love is blocked by: carnality, anger, resentment, jealousy, insecurity, impatience, morbidity, unresolved hurts, dislike, hyperactivity, tension, over-attachment, greed, pride, the negative, and obsession.

The real you is God's favorite person in the universe.

The real you is "wonderfully made" (*Psalm* 139:14).

It is radiant.

"Immediately a bright light surrounded me, filling the area where I stood," said Gladys L. Hargis of Topeka, Kansas, whose "glimpse" came in 2006. "It was beautiful beyond description, so beautiful that it took my breath away. I'm not certain I can find the right words to describe it. Standing in the light made me feel whole, pure, blessed, free, and loved. I felt I had just been born again into another realm, where I was completely at peace with my surroundings. Again, voices told me that I would live forever and never die, that only my body would be left behind, and that I would get a new body. Three more things were revealed: 1. There were no clocks in Heaven. My relatives would know when I was to come, and when I got there it would be as if I had been with them always. This was impressed upon me as a very important fact: Only on earth would I feel the pain of separation. In Heaven I would be just in another room. I could see relatives, friends, and family anytime I wanted. 2. There was no money or wealth to be brought with me, since it was of no value there. 3. My position on earth was of no importance, because I would be glorified in Heaven."

As a woman named Jules Lyons, who suffered a "horrible" accident in 1987, recalled, "I was slipping in and out of consciousness. Anyway, I remember the doctor's voice saying, 'There's nothing else we can do,' to someone, at the same moment I realized I had somehow floated upwards, out of my own body, and was moving toward the ceiling of the hospital room. I felt strangely, deeply calm, and incredibly peaceful . . . a sense of release . . . of immense freedom and lightness of being . . . It was simply the most amazing, beautiful thing I have ever, ever experienced . . . I felt an *overwhelming*, all-pervasive sense of deep, deep peace, joy, and calm . . . sheer calm, bliss, and peace . . . I found myself now floating along on what seemed to be thin air. Just clear, light, empty space; bright and clear, like crystal-clear air. I suddenly felt a rush of immense joy welling inside me, felt *so* uplifted and *so* peaceful and incredibly happy . . . I experienced what it felt like to feel truly free, as if every atom of my being was *free* and glowing with joy . . ."

There is vigor, youth, and health, but with maturity. "It is sown a perishable body, it is raised an imperishable body; it is sown in dishonor, it is raised in glory; it is sown in weakness, it is raised in power; it is sown a natural body, it is raised a spiritual body. If there is a natural body, there is also a spiritual body," says *1 Corinthians* 15:42-44.

You will possess an iridescence you never knew was within you.

It soars.

Luminosity comes from every part of the "body" and weaves in and out of other light, commensurate with the brightness of your "deep soul." It will be a body that is all light. Vision will be powerful—incredibly so, seeing all angles at once, and from great distances. Senses will have no limitations; there will be *additional* and radically new senses. There will be a hundred of them. Music will come, ministering, as if a breeze through the trees. You'll "hear" flowers blooming and bask in their fragrance as pleasure fills the lungs feeding beauty to the emotions and magnifying the sense of immeasurable well-being as you move as if on the wind.

What causes a feeling of wellness and peace on earth leads to the light of paradise.

What is in the spirit affects the body and after, in eternity, forms the atmosphere.

Thus, illness can be a warning (when not redemptive).

Nothing grows from soil that's unbalanced, that has the wrong "pH."

Extremes can plant us in purgatory.

Balance nurtures; extremes lead to sin.

If we have a disease caused by spiritual issues and we don't shake those spiritual issues they can follow us and require purgation. They are gone only when we have totally crossed through the veil, into the Light. There are those who can't seem to part with their afflictions. They refer to "my arthritis" or "my diabetes." You don't want to think of it like that. Take away the "my." That means you own it! It means you accept it. As an expert in this realm said, "When someone dies as a result of some illness then death does not automatically free them from the disease. After death they are still in the same way as they were when they were alive. Only when they pass through to the other side of death's curtain are they subjected to a cure. This, let us call it, 'quarantine' lasts just as long as the person's state demands. If their mental state demands a longer time, then that is what they get, till they are completely cured. It is treated individually, depending on the person's needs. If the person, for whatever reasons, resolves not to pass through to the Light, then they remain in the world of ghosts with all their mental and physical afflictions." And addictions. As Dr. Ritchie said, spirits in the "in-between" zone are there "until they solved whatever problem or difficulty was keeping them in that perplexed state." He saw a related area where people had realized their frame of mind, expressed repentance, let go of wrong desires, and (once these extremes were discarded), progressed toward the Light.

The soul that brings darkness (including self-pity, which is pride) paints the "walls" with it.

The soul that brings joy paints with light.

Cancel the "curse" that causes you tension.

It may be in your family tree.

Don't look *at* an obstacle. Look *over* it.

There is a ledger of positive and negative. It accompanies us. Our afterlife is as positive as we are. It's important to view everything in life from a positive perspective. When something negative occurs, think of the potential positive effects—for there always *are* positive aspects. When you think of those, you accent the positive power. Everything that occurs has a hidden treasure. When you think of a negative by piling on more negativity ("woe is me"), you activate it; you give it more force. You allow it to attach. These things add up, now and after. To focus on a negative is to give it energy. It has life. When it is given existence within us, it can manifest spiritually, psychologically, or physically. Repeating and mulling over and obsessing on negative issues or thoughts allows them to transform us in their likeness, instead of eradicating them. Life is a constant series of tests, and often it is between the two polar opposites of love and fear. We chose to love or to fear. When we fear, when we worry over everything, when anxiety is our normal response, we are not fearing death; we are fearing life! In so doing, we are wasting valuable time that could be spent loving, which brings contentment. Work your way toward joy. It comes with discipline. You may be addicted to negativity. The only way of halting that is to do the exact opposite.

Reconstruct—reverse—every negative thought pattern.

This will also "reverse the curse."

Pray every day: "Lord, lead me to everything I need to do to improve in this life and the one after."

It is the snake who seeks to bind us to this earth. You can hear his "hiss" in the words obsession, oppression, depression, and possession.

Any one of these indicates imbalance.

Imbalances can lead to infestations.

There is also *regression*.

There is transgression.

There is repression.

There is digression.

We get sidetracked.

Usually this is triggered by a problem or a series of unfortunate events.

When everything seems like it's falling around you, *let* it fall and watch how God builds something new with it.

It is a spiritual principle.

When we "let God," out of rubble comes grace.

Grace is Light and light does not tolerate darkness.

The darker it is, the brighter is that which bears light.

As a woman way back in the 1800s said, "We seem to think that the death of the body means an entire change to the soul. But this is not the case, by any means. We bring to the afterlife the same tastes, the same desires, the same knowledge we had before death. If these were not sufficiently pure and good to form a part of this life, then we ourselves may not enter. The purer the thoughts, the nobler the ambitions, the loftier the aspirations, the higher rank we take among the hosts of Heaven; the more earnestly we follow the studies and duties in our life of probation; the better fitted we shall be to carry them forward, on and on to completion and perfection."

We open that door with these words: *Jesus, Jesus, Jesus.*

Added the Seattle experiencer: "It is important for us to acquire knowledge of the spirit while we are in the flesh. The more knowledge we acquire here, the further and faster we will progress there. Because of lack of knowledge or belief, some spirits are virtual prisoners of this earth."

The kinds of lives we live and the thoughts we think and the prayers we say from the heart decide not just where but *how* we reside in the initial place of "forever."

On the other side are various settings.

There are abodes in that countryside, near inconceivable waterfalls, in those grand, expansive "forests," next to pastures, in hamlets. There are cottages. There are hovels. There are mansions (many: *John* 14:2). There are villages and towns and cities of light and "cities" within those cities. I read an account of a Chinese woman who had passed on after a long illness and walked with Jesus to gates of pearl which were opened by angels past which she saw gorgeously colored houses and golden streets. When Rebecca Springer had her extensive near-death experience (which was back in the 1800s), she visited the home that her brother had helped construct for her.

When she asked about small homes, he replied, "That was all the material (good works) they sent up."

To repeat: Your mission is your mansion.

Your true purpose brings you closer to God.

Use what you are given to *give* to others (and your gifts will grow).

The more you give, the more of God's Grace will flow through you—healing here on earth; registering in Heaven.

Death is no more traumatic, to those prepared, than leaving one room and entering another.

"Let me tell you, my dear friends, there is always an angel with you as you leave this world," said Gladys. "If you love everyone as yourself, the heavens will open up and receive you. But be aware. If you are evil with evil thoughts, you will never see the light or the cleansing white cloud that washes away the old earth and makes you pure, to be able to see the Lord."

A pure heart is a portal to God.

It holds nothing back.

It bears no secret.

Look at negative trends that keep repeating in your life and tackle them.

Life is about how you *do* things, your tone of voice, the pattern of your thoughts.

With discipline, every thought that was critical can be turned into a kind one.

(As soon as a person enters your thoughts, pray for him. In this way there will not be a negative perspective.)

The virtues are always with us. So is perseverance. Remember that the seer from Kibeho called purgatory the "place of those who persevere."

"The Lord will give people situations, like cancer," adds a woman named Lisa Tesch. "They're scared. They're so frightened. They have no idea what they're going to run into or what to expect to happen. All I can say is, 'Rejoice!' When you are embraced in the Arms of the Father Almighty, there is no greater Presence. And it's total, holy, pure love. He totally embraces you and you become one in Him. I said, 'Jesus, save me,' and I was instantly in His Presence."

Death dissolves like a vapor.

If we fail to use our faith and help others we are like the Pharisees who castigated Jesus for violating the "law" of the Sabbath by healing the blind man.

Who was without sight: the blind man or the Pharisees?

There is "over-scrupulosity."

We can't see the forest for the trees.

We are "penny wise and pound foolish."

We lose sight of the "big picture."

God is merciful—hugely. We must never forget this! You cannot imagine His kindness.

Extremes distort our emotions.

When Angie Fenimore had her experience she learned that "hell, while also a specific dimension, is primarily a state of mind. When we die, we are bound by what we think. In mortality the more solid our thoughts become, as we act upon them—allowing darkness to develop in others, and in ourselves—the more damning they are."

This distraught young mother (who if we recall attempted suicide) had "landed on the edge of a shadowy plane, suspended in the darkness, extending to the limits of my sight. Its floor was firm but shrouded in black mist, swirling around my feet, that also formed the thick, waist-high barrier that held me prisoner. The place was charged with a crackling energy that sparked me into hyper-alertness, a state of hair-trigger sensitivity. Again, I perceived my surroundings not through physical sensations but through a kind of telepathic intuition. The fog-like mist had mass—it seemed to be formed of molecules of intense darkness—and it could be handled and shaped." The others there "were completely self-absorbed, every one of them too caught up in his or her own misery to engage in any mental or emotional exchange," she added.

"I had been in hell long before I died," Fenimore went on, "and I hadn't realized it because I had escaped many of the consequences up until the point that I took my life. But when we die, our state of mind grows far more obvious because we are gathered together with those who think as we do. As I watched them filing in by the dozens, I was told that most of us who are dying now are going to a place of darkness."

When Saint Anthony the hermit saw how many snares there are in the world, he called out, "Who can ever escape so many dangers?" and heard a Voice say, *"Anthony, humility alone walks securely; he who goes with head bowed down, need not fear to fall into these snares."*

Chapter 18

"Indeed, the devil is working in the interest of hell when he inspires a soul with a desire for the esteem of the world," wrote Saint Alphonsus. "For when a soul loses humility it runs the risk of being hurled into the abyss."

"The less we have here, the greater will be our joy in Heaven, where our dwelling shall correspond to the love with which we imitated the life of our Divine Master here on earth," said Saint Teresa of Avila.

It is through discipline that we control wrong thoughts, replacing them swiftly with right ones and it is through the same discipline that *anything* can be removed that might darken us, that might hold us back.

Discipline prepares us for eternity.

Heaven is discipline combined with freedom because true discipline frees you.

Joy comes even in adversity.

When we're disciplined in one thing, we grow disciplined in others.

Start with whatever you can.

Just persist.

God doesn't expect you to be perfect. This place called earth seems impossible!

He wants *effort*.

Persist and the bad habits, the darkness, will flee from you.

Simply hold a light in the murkiness.

(This is the key: *just hold up the lamp of love.*)

"All of the people who go through this come away believing that the most important thing in their life is love," said a very prominent researcher of death experiences. "For most of them, the second most important thing in life is knowledge. As they see life scenes in which they are learning things, the Being points out that one of the things they can take with them at death is knowledge."

The more we know about the afterlife, the faster we advance.

We move quickest with knowledge of Jesus.

We advance with Our Blessed Mother.

"Happy is the death of one who is calling upon Mary!" said a commentator. "In those supreme moments one's prayer to Our Lady draws down the heavenly comfort of feeling the presence of the Mother of all mercy. When one loves Our Lady, the recollection of that love gives him a filial confidence that he will be saved. St. Madeleine Sophie Barat in her pleasing way said, 'The death of one truly devoted to Mary is a child's leap into his mother's arms.'"

St. Bonaventure wrote that "devoutly invoking the Virgin is a sign of salvation."

At Kibeho the Blessed Mother said, "What are you waiting for? You spend your time indulging yourselves in worldly pleasure, whereas eternal happiness belongs to the one who has known suffering, accepted it, and offered it up to the Lord. Travelers! Why look back? What have you left behind? Take your luggage now because the remaining road is short.

"Look forward because happiness lies in front of you."

So strong were these lessons that one of the seers consented to the trial of praying in the jungle as a leopard threatened and at times clawed at her.

We are here to learn and when we fail we must go at it once more instead of hovering over the failure (which is what the enemy wants).

Pick yourself up by the bootstraps.

Don't accept the evil report. What is an "evil report"? You have disease. You are going to die. You will never get out of debt. God alone knows. Does He answer every prayer? Only if it goes toward your purpose. He answers in four ways: yes, no, I can't hear you, wait. Or—if we are faithful to Him—He simply removes our obsession with what may not be in His Plan for us.

On the verge of a second Heisman Trophy (as top player in college football, a rare feat), and feeling the immense pressure, a quarterback named Archie Griffin turned to the Bible and it was there that he located advice for his troubled mind. It was in Psalm 37 ("Take delight in the Lord, and He will give you the desires of your heart.") "I read that verse and it was like someone lifted a great weight off of my shoulders because it told me that my job was to find joy and be who I am and serving the Lord. And if I would do that, the Lord will do one of two things: He'll give me the trophy as a gift or He would take away that desire I had of wanting to win it."

He did win, against all odds.

"My life on earth would be prolonged, I understood, by living so as to be in a helping capacity—helping others," said Elane Durham.

No doctor or lawyer or professor—not anyone—knows what God does.

Case in point: in 1958, Saint Padre Pio was terribly afflicted by bronchial pneumonia—prostrated by it. It wouldn't leave, despite best efforts. Early in May, they called his illness "pleurisy" and ordered absolute bed rest. Nothing worked. "After May 5, he was confined to his room, unable to celebrate Mass or hear Confessions," recounts Bernard Ruffin in one of the very best books on this saint (*Padre Pio: The True Story*). "Three times during May, Pio's physicians drew more than a quart of bloody fluid from his pleural cavities without bringing relief. Padre Carmelo of Sessano, the guardian, summoned well-known specialists. After making various tests, they arrived at a grim diagnosis: 'pleural neoplasm with bloody exudations.' They recommended a terrible regimen of chemotherapy. With solemn faces, three doctors entered Pio's room and told him that he had cancer and had no more than a few months to live. To their shock, the sick man burst out laughing and told them they did not know what they were talking about." Pio refused chemotherapy but remained infirm. But on August 5 of that year (the Feast of Our Lady of the Snows, and also thought by many to be her actual birthday), the famous international pilgrim statue from Fatima was brought by helicopter to that part of Italy and for several days the faithful prayed. It was also brought to the church at Pio's monastery—where, despite his illness, Saint Pio was carried to the sanctuary and managed to kneel before the image and drape a golden rosary around it. Afterward, breathless and in pain, he was carried back to bed. But a miracle was about to occur. Pio had not accepted the "evil report." "When the statue was being conveyed away by helicopter, Pio murmured, 'Dear Mother, ever since you came to Italy, I have been immobilized by sickness. Now that you're leaving, aren't you going to say even a word to me?'" wrote

Ruffin. And: "In the twinkling of an eye, the padre felt 'a mysterious force' surge through his body. Immediately he shouted, 'I'm healed!' and leaped from his bed. Pio felt completely cured. Within two weeks he had resumed all his duties."

The Blessed Mother can provide you a way out of situations that have "no exit"—at least that you can see.

When Kathy Latrelle had her brush with eternity in 1979, she was shown the benchmarks that changed her life. She was shown points at which she could have become embittered, but chose not to. She was shown times she'd helped others, which was of the utmost importance to God. She also glimpsed her future as a winding path that stretched out below. "Some sections of the path glowed in brilliant colors, every color of the spectrum," noted authors Lionel C. Bascom and Barbara Loecher. "At its brightest, the path was a glowing yellow. In sections the yellow gave way to brilliant, glowing orange, then red, then violet, and finally a deep blue and black. Kathy understood that the bright sections were times of joy in her life; the dark, times of loss and pain. She saw the beginning of her path, and knew this was her life in her twenties, with the dark spots and light spots. Her thirties were a gradient of color, starting with a long swath of bright yellow, then turning blue and finally black. The path remained black for a while, before growing lighter again. She knew the dark section would be a time of terrible loss and death. The path stretched on through her forties, fifties, and sixties. She wasn't sure she would live through her early eighties. She understood that there would be pain along the way, but there was also great joy."

Often, the dark colors come through our choices.

You can be diverted from a direct route to your mission.

Some go directly, on the surface. Some are "under water" for a while. Some scrape along the muddy bottom, or divert along the shore. But you finally reach a certain point and your time is up. God is more concerned with how and where that is than how you got there.

Everything can be worked for the *good* when we let it.

It's how we make it.

It's how we take it.

When we divert too much, we subtract from what we were assigned to do.

This is wisdom, which you take with you. It is part of your identity.

Seek wisdom and the truth of who you are and what you must do will come to you, for wisdom is truth (where knowledge can be interpreted various ways).

As Pope Francis said, "The first gift of the Holy Spirit is wisdom. It is not merely human wisdom, no, the fruit of knowledge and experience. Obviously this gift comes from intimacy with God. For our intimate relationship with God. From our relationship as children with a Father. And the Holy Spirit – when we have this relationship – gives us the gift of wisdom. When we are in communion with the Lord, it is as if the Spirit transfigures our heart and helps it to perceive all His warmth and predilection. The Holy Spirit also makes the Christian 'wise.' This is, however, not in the sense that he or she has an answer for everything, or knows everything, but in the sense that he or she 'knows' of God, how God acts, they know when something is of God and when it is not. They know this, they have this wisdom that God gives our heart. The heart of the wise man has this taste of God. We have the Holy Spirit in our hearts; we can listen to him or not. If we listen to Him He teaches us this path of wisdom, He gifts us wisdom which is seeing with God's eyes, listening with God's ears, loving with God's Heart, judging things with God's judgment."

Those enamored of their own "knowledge" or "intelligence" will one day learn the severe limits to them (and no human way to test them). They will learn that they didn't know what they knew. They will be surprised at how they had blinded themselves.

Blindness comes with each wrong thought.

So, blindness comes with worldliness. We can't see when we are in front of ourselves. There is a surgeon from India named Rajiv Parti. He left his body during a bladder procedure. What he saw changed his life—a dark place filled with a great wild fire and lightning all around. There, he realized his sins. He was not kind to his patients. They were a means of making money. When he met someone, he always asked, "What can I get from this person?" He was especially harsh toward those he perceived to be lower in social or professional status. He saw how many people he had used and how many toes he'd stepped on to get ahead, remembering one elderly woman with arthritis. "She wanted to talk to me," he told a newspaper. "She wanted a little touch on the shoulder, because her husband was dying of cancer." Instead, Dr. Parti dashed off a prescription and walked swiftly from the room. In the hellish realm, this caused him great sorrow, and when he returned he sold his Hummer, Mercedes, and ten-thousand-square-foot house.

We are meant to be those "who walk not according to the flesh but according to the Spirit" (*Romans* 8:4).

Grasp each precious moment of life. Each counts. Purify it.

To prepare for Heaven, to purify here, and keep pure, do, say, and think everything in the Presence of God.

Think always of His Presence.

In every single act, see Him as your audience.

Don't bring guilt, loneliness, inferiority, insecurity, depression, addiction, or *self-assessment* that is overly harsh.

There is no need, if you have tried, at least, to be with Christ.

When the "council" judges you, you will be surprised by their softness, wisdom, and love.

"My guide took me by the arm and led me to a room where the judges were sitting at a rectangular table," said another of the millions who have died and returned. "They were all dressed in loose white garments. I sensed their age and wisdom. In their company, I felt quite boyish."

"They radiated a benevolent type of caring; my fear left me," says another.

"Although I felt unworthy, it seemed the balance was in my favor and, throughout all these scenes from my life, good and bad, I received the same sense of great love," said a woman named René. "While all these events [of my life] were being played, I never felt judged. All I felt was my own guilt burdening me. Seeing this, the ever-loving gatekeeper directed me to look at kindnesses I had done, the acts of concern for others. I saw lives I'd saved or tried to save as a lifeguard and ambulance officer."

To endure is to triumph.

Self-pity is self-defeating.

Toss aside the irrelevant.

Pray for the benefit of everyone.

Remember that "those souls are quickest to enter Heaven who quickly sense their sins, who are not obstinately taken up with their own self-conceit," said the revelation from 1931. "God judges us, not according to our failings, but according to our good will. A soul who is always ready to recognize God's Will and to do it is indeed by that very fact good. Such a soul does not quickly take offense when somebody reminds it of its failings, and tries in a spirit of great joy, pleasure, and gratitude to overcome and lay aside this or that fault."

As Saint John XXIII added, "The surest way to my personal sanctification is the constant effort to reduce everything—principles, objectives, position, business—to the utmost simplicity and tranquility; to always prune my vineyard of useless leaves and tendrils and concentrate on truth, justice, and charity, but above all charity. Every other way of acting is pretension and a search for personal affirmation, which soon reveals itself as absurd and burdensome. I consider it a sign the great Mercy of the Lord Jesus has for me that He continues to give His peace and external signs of grace as well, which, I am told, explain the resilience of my calm, making me enjoy, in every hour of my day, a simplicity and gentleness of spirit that keep me ready to leave all and set off at a moment's notice for eternal life."

The simpler we are, the smaller; the smaller, the easier through a narrow entrance.

This brings peace.

For the most part, we are serene at death. The sacraments are invaluable.

"I felt no pain as I seemed to lift higher and higher; it became dark and I was still traveling rapidly," said a fifty-year-old woman, recounting her "death" at age eleven when she was struck by a car. "There was an overwhelming sense of being loved, like the whole universe loved me. I came to a stop in front of some sort of barrier which looked like a privet hedge."

Beyond this are loved ones with whom we will traverse eons.

It will be: a constant unfolding of the present.

Heaven is now. It is timeless. All of your tomorrows are God's yesterdays.

If there are no churches it is because it is *direct adoration*. It does so well to practice that here!

There is only "time" to praise Him.

Desire this with all your heart and you will get to Heaven.

Wrote a woman named Elizabeth Pringle of a near-death brush as a toddler (like others, she could remember even at such a young age): "I was twenty-two months old in Clydebank, Scotland. We had just been through the Blitz. As a result of being dragged out of bed in dark of night, seeking underground shelter, I contracted pneumonia. Penicillin was not yet available, the fever would not break, the priest was called. I was thought to be 'gone' when he arrived. He anointed me and administered the Last Rites. I saw the Lord. To me He was a Star, the most beautiful star I had ever seen, way up in the darkness. I started to run to him. 'No,' He said, 'you must go back. My Father has work for you.' Crushed, I reluctantly obeyed. For many years this encounter was buried in the annals of time yet its still unfolding ramifications have affected my entire life. There is nothing on earth to compete with the power of the Sacraments in God's Holy Church. Death has no sway over God's perfect Will but I had to obey or I would have missed all of the incredible life I have been allotted. Destiny hangs by the finest of threads."

Chapter 19

Sense your mission in life—and go for it.

Bless those who curse you.

Trials that are handled with joy end in glory.

"When you bless, you become ready to receive blessing," noted a priest.

When someone aggravates you, "drink not of the poison."

Remember: the more God takes away, the more you're left with.

Choose the right "door" and win the secret petitions of your heart.

A pruned tree bears more fruit. Prune.

Pray to know the "truth of the moment."

When negativity comes, put up a "no vacancy" sign.

To hover on a hurt is to give it power (even unto death).

Rid yourself of past injuries. Let them go!

The bigger your problem, the bigger your destiny.

Clear the secret chambers of your soul.

Don't look back at Sodom.

View life from the tallest branch.

Maintain the high point of your life.

If you are right with God, why would you care what others think?

Breathe the living waters—before you even get to them.

Bring with you *great expectations*.

Cast out darkness by finding *the rhythm of faith*.

See one miracle occur, then another, then another.

Talk *to* the mountain (not about it).

Aim for joy (not excitement).

Pray always to see the big picture.

When things don't go as planned, remember: it could be God stirring up the pot.

Bad things are only bad when they bear no lesson.

Make sure there is no darkness.

Call this a "law of the crows": Around you are spirits that want to trip you up. The devil often tries to divert our attention and often does so—at crucial moments—as we near a threshold. Often he works against us in the way of a sideshow. He comes at the periphery. He is barely in view. He seeks only to shift your glance long enough to cause mayhem (a wrong decision). Often we recognize evil when it causes us anxiety or depression or anger or even rage—when it divides us, when it slanders, when we regress spiritually, when there is confusion, and turmoil, when it leads to sin—but just as often the devil attacks through distraction. I was driving one day and suddenly a crow bounded on the street and then another hopped in a strange manner on the other side of the pavement, as if to grab my attention. The temptation was to abruptly look their way, which could have caused an accident, which at the least would have been a great *disruption*. There was two-way traffic, and I was approaching a turn—as in life we approach crossroads that lead or don't lead to holiness, that lead or don't lead to spiritual advancement. It especially happens when there is a decision or move or commitment to make. He is the great deceiver and a ploy of a deceiver is misdirection. Crossroads. When we approach a threshold, something interferes (if we let it). Evil is where evil lies and so one must watch at the periphery for what is peculiar, what's artificial, what's too spectacular, what is unbalanced, what causes despair, what leads to procrastination. Evil is where you find falsehood. It has a sales pitch. It is diversionary. Satan is a liar and he lies in wait (like the snake that he is). Don't expect him to come in a way that is obvious. Watch for his suddenness. Be alert to what glimmers. How many times has the devil diverted you? How many times has he made you pay attention to something trivial when there were more important matters? How much time and energy has he caused you to waste? How many instances are there where you failed to note a problem or missed opportunities because you were paying attention to something other than what you should have? We all have intersections in life (more than we realize) and we approach them in the right fashion when we are looking (through prayer) straight ahead. The cock crows thrice; the crow caws.

"Satan is a master of illusion," says Betty. "He mirrors life, creating false images that deceive even the most astute. He cleverly counterfeits true principles and holds false ones up for admiration. For example, he convinces many that the riches of the world are a means of freedom. Riches, however, weigh us down with the responsibility to properly manage them. They do offer means to bless others if we diligently learn how to use them in wisdom. But wealth in the hands of the unprepared and unwise becomes a millstone, dragging the rich by the neck into greed, confusion, dissipation, and eventual misery.

"Satan can disguise himself as an angel of light, appearing to be the answer when in fact he is the problem.

Fortunately, a false spirit posing as an angel of light casts a long, dark shadow. That is the nature of evil. It is a tree that bears bitter fruit that can always be detected over time. Evil will take on any form necessary to tempt us, to test us, to claim us, hoping we don't look too closely at its real composition. Satan uses negative energies to deceive us into choosing doors or routes which lead into his realm. Damning the consequences, we enter the world of consensual darkness where Satan blinds us with ever greater deception, drawing us in deeper and convincing us to remain. Once enslaved, we turn our backs on God until our pain is so great that we frantically look for relief."

This is where the pits are. It then takes intervention of God, Jesus, and angels to draw us out. There is an account on the internet of a man whose body lapsed into clinical death during a swimming accident and who followed a torch he saw in the distance that turned into a fiery place where a horrid creature with a head like a bull sat atop a massive pile of jewelry and tarnished gold.

He is the great deceiver who uses our fears to hold us captive.

Fear is the opposite of love.

His domain is that of *unlove.* He taunts. He whispers. He tries to have us think his thoughts are our own. In this way he diverts us or outright stops us in our tracks.

There are times that God blocks us. It is not the devil. There are times we are headed the wrong way and the Lord tries to nudge us in the right one. This we must discern. But it can also be the evil one and of course he does not only use crows. He sends people to block us, to place a trench, to put up a stop sign, where we are not meant to stop. The attacks often come from those who are familiar to us and thus in a way, again, we don't expect. Look at how an apostle—Peter—tried to divert Jesus!

Too often, we let others make the decisions for us.

This also is a problem at "intersections." This too the devil sends. Look straight ahead and always turn back to your direct path when something crops up on the side of you. Let Jesus be your guide, always. When it happened to Him, with Peter, He said, "Get thee hence!" *Approach every day* with the Rosary—firmly—and the devil will lose this device. Turn the tables. Use adversity to sharpen your virtues. In prayer you will spot the diversions. Look for the Good Lord's Light in prayer and remember that His Light does not divert because His light does not bend.

Chapter 20

Yet, light surrounds us.

We bring this above all else: light, the brightness of our being, which reflects our purity at the end of life.

Attendant to accounts of death are those descriptions of a parting luminosity—and not just by the person dying.

"I saw this film or transparent envelope of light close up and lift her 'body' going upwards and out of sight," said a man who watched his mother pass.

The brightest light "I'd ever seen," was the way another described an inexplicable illumination.

When his grandfather died, one young man reported a "golden ball of light" lift from his chest and pass through the ceiling, according to a researcher.

Mists. Rays. Tiny light particles. That globe.

In 1963, two coal miners near Hazleton, Pennsylvania, found themselves trapped with no hope of escape. In all, they spent fourteen days entombed far below the surface as rescuers frantically tried to reach them. They both testified that for the last week of this ordeal, *Pope John XXIII appeared in the cave*, illuminating it with a bluish light that radiated from him. The apparition had followed "three tiny bluish fireflies" that "suddenly appeared in the total darkness" and "began expanding and soon filled the entire chamber with a bluish light," according to an account.

As in near-death stories, the Pope looked younger than when he had died a short ten weeks before and wore simple attire: a surplice and cassock. He said nothing—just remained as a consoling presence to which both men testified in great detail, not only agreeing with each other in every regard concerning the apparition but passing polygraph examinations and the scrutiny of psychologists.

One of the miners, David Fellin, testified that the bluish light, which cast no shadow, "had provided perfect visibility. He also said the small enclosure where they had been trapped expanded, enabling them to move around. Fellin further testified that, when the bluish light enabled them to see, he noticed Pope John XXIII at an elevation in the distance, visible only from the waist up. He said the pontiff, who was 81 when he died, appeared to be about half that age; his arms were folded in front of him; and he was grinning at them."

Consolation—and assistance (light)—come in many ways.

Everyone passes into eternity alone—*and yet doesn't.*

"The day my mother died, my two brothers, my sister, my sister-in-law, and I were all in the room," a woman from Atlanta told the author of a book called *Glimpses of Eternity*. "My mother hadn't spoken a word in several hours, and she was breathing in an irregular pattern. None of us were really upset because mother had been on a downhill course and we knew this was the end.

"Suddenly, a bright light appeared in the room. My first thought was that a reflection was shining through the window from a vehicle passing by outside. Even as I thought that, however, I knew it wasn't true, because this was not any kind of light on this earth. I nudged my sister to see if she saw it too, and when I looked at her, her eyes were as big as saucers. At the same time I saw my brother literally gasp. Everyone saw it together. Then my mother just expired and we all kind of breathed a sigh of relief. At that moment, we saw vivid bright lights that seemed to gather around and shape up into—I don't know what to call it, except an entranceway. Being by it was a feeling of complete joy."

A Canadian doctor related an episode during which he spotted a patient standing down a hall staring at something. The man was strangely illuminated. Approaching, the doctor realized that his patient, who had severe chronic obstructive pulmonary disease, was in spirit looking at his own body—his corpse—on a gurney! He had died. "There was a light of sorts that emanated from him—a clear light—and I felt like I was seeing his soul," said the doctor.

In a "flash," the patient disappeared in a field of "bright golden light."

There was a sense of joyful energy rolling back and forth, as if unseen presences had been there to assist.

Our angels go every step of the way with us!

"When patients spoke of angels—which many did—the angels were always described as more beautiful than they had ever imagined, eight feet tall, male, and wearing a white for which there is no word," wrote a registered nurse, Trudy Harris. Most people seemed to receive exactly what they need to hear or see to die peacefully. "I saw a medium-sized person standing at my right hand clothed in white with a bright countenance, beaming with intelligence," a railroad worker from Jacksonville, Florida, told researchers. "I knew what he wanted in an instant, although he put his hand on my shoulder and said, 'Come with me.'"

Said an Australian woman who had her experience in the 1980s, "I saw a bright light; it became clearer and an arched doorway appeared and slowly opened. In the background were many angels and one moved forward and spoke to me but his mouth never moved. His voice went right into my heart and said, *'Jenny, I am coming for you.'* He truly looked beautiful, like a king—dressed in a white flowing gown and a royal blue cloak."

"It's amazing," said Gladys Hargis. "The angels are with you from the beginning to the end of your journey. They welcome you in song, rejoicing with an outpouring love. You never feel alone or afraid. You are drawn to their power, and yet they only guide you. You want to follow them because the love they give you is so overwhelming. It is more of a chant, like a beckoning on the breeze."

Our angels go with us and take us on the tour of forever.

Other times, Jesus or relatives do. In one study, deceased relatives were the most frequently mentioned aspect of such an experience. If they are not there just before the transition, they are after!

Trapped in a burning car after a horrible head-on collision, a woman named Tracey Stadler desperately prayed. *"Please don't let me burn to death."* Then she looked up; and there he was. "When I say 'he' it was a person who I knew wasn't of this world," she told a Christian network. "It was a Heaven-sent person in an angelic form. And at that point he just lifted me up and I went with him. He pulled me out and we started getting further away from the accident site. At that point I know I left my body. I know I did. He told me I could look back if I wanted to, but I didn't want to. And the further we got away from the accident site the more peace I felt—such peace. And the love? The love can't be explained; we're too finite in our words. It can't be explained in human terms. The love, like you are going home. There was no pain, no regret, only anticipation. The only thing that mattered was my relationship with Christ. And I felt like I was in the arms of God, of Jesus Christ himself," she said, adding that they ascended into what seemed like paradise, where she encountered a grandmother who had died when she was a little girl.

"And I was so thrilled to see her and she was thrilled to see me," Tracey recounted. "She knew me and I knew her right away. I started to go toward her and I stopped and I said, 'Megan!' That's our oldest daughter who was nine months old at the time. And I said, 'I have to go back.' I mean, I *knew* I was going to see the Face of God. I knew it. But I couldn't let Megan grow up alone. And we started going down, and this was just the opposite of going up. It was hard. It was cold. It was fast, and it was painful coming back."

When we are still needed, we return. Only on the other side will we understand how God orchestrates it. This much we can say: prayers of desperation pierce the clouds and angels or deceased loved ones are assigned to assist at a speed that is instant.

"I noticed a light coming into my room," said a girl whose experience occurred when she was just four. "It was a beautiful golden-white light which seemed to appear in the wall to the left of my bed. I sat up and watched the light grow. It grew rapidly in both size and brightness. In fact the light got so bright that it seemed to me that the whole world was being lit up by it. I could see someone inside the light. There was this beautiful woman, and she was part of the light: in fact she glowed. Her body was lit from the inside. It seemed as if she was a pure crystal filled with light. Even her robe glowed with a light as if by itself. She called me by name and held out her hand to me. She told me to come with her. Her voice was very soft and gentle. I asked her who she was and she said she was my guardian and had been sent to take me to a place where I could rest in peace. The love emanating from her washed over me so that I did not hesitate to put my hand in hers."

A nine-year-old boy recalled going through a dark tunnel and being met on the other side by a group of angels.

Said another little girl, "They don't fly; they just come!"

When Deborah Shambora was struck by a horse, she encountered Jesus in an intensive-care unit.

Since then, she told a television interviewer, she frequently has been able to see the supernatural dimension.

"Just recently I was in California ministering and I could see a woman directly in front of me and she had her head in her hands and her husband was stroking her jacket. And the Lord said to me, *'That woman has a severe migraine headache, but it's an attack by the enemy. He doesn't want her to hear what will be spoken.'* So I said, 'Okay, Lord, what would you have me do?' And He said, *'Start interceding and praying for her.'* So I did and then I saw an angel come down the aisle and he was carrying a pitcher and he walked over to her and he poured an oily-watery substance on her, an anointing, and within thirty seconds she just sat straight up in her chair and was totally involved in the service and felt great. I could tell."

It reminds us of the Anointing of the Sick (and statues that exude healing oil).

"There are literally legions of angels that are at the disposal of the Holy Spirit on our behalf," wrote Richard Sigmund. "I saw millions and millions of angels for every purpose that God has intended in Heaven. But I was not allowed to see all of them. I knew there were other areas of Heaven where I could not go and there were other classes of angels that I was not allowed to see—different types. I saw angels that were in charge of the weather and angels that were in charge of protection. Some of them were clothed with the power to move earth."

According to Reverend Storm (who had that hellish brush, but was rescued by Jesus, Who put him in the company of angels): "Angels rarely appear in their glory. The times that angels have appeared to me in their full glory it was almost unbearable. The brightness of the light that radiates from them is brighter than the light from a welder's torch. Their light doesn't burn the eye, but it is frightening because it is so different from our experience of life. They don't appear to us in their natural state very often. They most often tone it down for us to keep comfortable. I don't have the words adequately to describe angels in their natural state. Brighter than lightning, beautiful beyond comparison, powerful, loving, and gentle are words that fail to describe them. The artists' depictions of angels are pitifully inadequate. How do you paint something that is more radiant than substance? How do you paint colors that you have never seen before or since? The angels are with us constantly and they are everywhere. We are never apart from them. We have angels who guard us from evil. Why they intervene sometimes and other times don't is between them and God. God wants us to experience the consequence of our actions. On special rare occasions God allows the angels to help. When we ask God for spiritual gifts of love, faith, and hope, God always allows the angels to help us. Spiritual gifts are never refused if we are ready to receive them. The angels are working all the time to give us the Love of God, faith in God, hope in God. Angels hear our prayers."

The accounts of miracles associated with them are endless.

I have seen remarkable occurrences. I have heard of cars that should have killed people but didn't because the vehicle seemed to go right through them (or their vehicle) at the last second, as if reality, and metal, had liquefied. I have seen twisted automobile wreckage that had the form of angels or deceased—in a tangle of debris where folks survived but should not have. I've heard stories about mysterious strangers appearing at horrendous scenes and orchestrating a rescue. I have read reliable instances where hands from nowhere seemed to lift a car or truck that was crushing a person or to reach in a window and pull someone out of a car or a flaming house. I have seen fascinating photographs of "reflections" that took the form of towering heavenly entities, sometimes winged, on the ceiling of a church (during a funeral Mass) or in a hospital ward where a child was miraculously healed. As Storm further explicated, "There are different kinds of angels with different responsibilities and different attributes. One angel may accompany a child, another has responsibility for a city, another a nation. The Spirit of God is the spirit of angels. This same Spirit is in us leading us to truth and love. When we allow the Holy Spirit to guide us, we are in harmony with the angels and God."

It is this harmony—and cleanliness—that traverse with us, that pave our path.

Note how "immaculate" Mary was. Note how clear and luminous angels are said to be. We die into our cleanliness, our clarity, and the clearer we are, the brighter the reality around us. To seek clarity is a chore of our lives; it is a constant war; every day, dirt is kicked up to sully or blind us. The devil creates dustdevils. He is tornadic. The word "hurricane" comes from the Indian word for "evil spirit" (*hurucan*). The less grit we have, the farther we see now as well as later. I recall a woman in Austria (with royal lineage: she was a princess) and her encounters with souls who bore the characteristics of their sin: bedraggled, or blackened, or with the features of various beasts, in accordance with their interior condition.

Wrong tendencies energize demons, who attack every virtue.

"Angels are aware of and protect us from forces we don't know or aren't capable of imagining," wrote Dr. Storm. "There exist supernatural beings that seek chaos. They have no power over us except the power we give them. Our angels are ever vigilant to protect us from evil that originates in other dimensions."

When the Seattle woman returned from Heaven, demons tried to attack her, but her guardians placed a bubble of protection over her, frustrating their feverish attempt to climb up and get to her.

"They appeared to be half-human half-animal—short, muscular beings with long claws or fingernails and savage, though human, faces," she wrote, explaining how five such creatures entered her room at the hospital. "They came to me, snarling, growling, and hissing. They were full of hate, and I knew that they intended to kill me. I tried to scream but was either too weak or too paralyzed with fear to move. I was helpless as they came to within five or six feet of the bed. Suddenly, a huge dome of light, almost like glass, fell over me, and the creatures lunged forward, seeming to recognize its threat to them. The dome protected me as they frantically flailed at it and tried to climb on it to get a better vantage point. But the dome was too high to climb on, and they became more frustrated. They shrieked and cursed and hissed and began spitting. When I thought I could bear it no more and my fear seemed about to overwhelm me, my three adoring angels [who looked like monks] entered the room again, and the creatures fled."

She was told that it's important for us to gain spiritual knowledge while we are in the flesh. For the more knowledge of the spirit we acquire, the further and faster we will progress in the hereafter. Some, she said, because of lack of belief or knowledge, are "virtual prisoners" of this earth.

Some who die as atheists, or those who have bonded to the world through greed, bodily appetites, or other earthly commitments find it difficult to move on, and they become earthbound, she added. "They often lack the faith and power to reach for, or in some cases even to recognize, the energy and light that pulls us toward God. These spirits stay on earth until they learn to accept the greater power around them and to let go of the world. When I was in the black [tunnel] before heading towards the light, I felt the presence of such lingering spirits."

I recently viewed an interview with a physician from Oklahoma who found himself in a nether place because he was too "learned" to believe in God—didn't need Him, until he was on his deathbed.

There, it seems, one learns quickly.

"Why, then, do you fear to take up the Cross when through it you can win a kingdom?" wrote Thomas á Kempis.

"In the Cross is salvation, in the Cross is life, in the Cross is protection from enemies, in the Cross is infusion of heavenly sweetness, in the Cross is strength of mind, in the Cross is joy of spirit, in the Cross is highest virtue, in the Cross is perfect holiness. There is no salvation of soul nor hope of everlasting life but in the Cross.

"Take up your cross, therefore, and follow Jesus, and you shall enter eternal life. He Himself opened the way before you in carrying His Cross, and upon it He died for you, that you, too, might take up your cross and long to die upon it. If you die with Him, you shall also live with Him, and if you share His suffering, you shall also share His glory.

"Behold, in the Cross is everything, and upon your dying on the Cross everything depends. There is no other way to life and to true inward peace than the way of the holy Cross and daily mortification. Go where you will, seek what you will, you will not find a higher way, nor a less exalted but safer way, than the way of the holy Cross. Arrange and order everything to suit your will and judgment, and still you will find that some suffering must always be borne, willingly or unwillingly, and thus you will always find the cross. When you shall have come to the point where suffering is sweet and acceptable for the sake of Christ, then consider yourself fortunate, for you have found paradise on earth. But as long as suffering irks you and you seek to escape, so long will you be unfortunate, and the tribulation you seek to evade will follow you everywhere. If you put your mind to the things you ought to consider, that is, to suffering and death, you would soon be in a better state and would find peace. No man is fit to enjoy Heaven unless he has resigned himself to suffer hardship for Christ. Realize that you must lead a dying life; the more a man dies to himself, the more he begins to live unto God. Nothing is more acceptable to God, nothing more helpful for you on this earth than to suffer willingly for Christ. 'If any man will come after Me, let him deny himself, and take up his cross daily, and follow Me.'"

On the cross we crucify our egos. From its height, we see.

What we crucify, what we place upon our "crosses," will purify. This brings joy here and later!

The more we die to self, the more we live.

The more we reach joy, the more surrounds us—joy in every circumstance, at each turn, beyond every threshold.

Thus in our thoughts always should be: patience, sacrifice, joy, love, kindness. This is the recipe for tranquility. Pursue these.

Tranquility is a taste of paradise.

Step through this threshold!

Remember at the same time: suffering can be caused by the enemy (often *is*) and demons must be cast off.

No one needs them at bedside.

They are not light; they are shining darkness.

Jesus has total power over them, when we are near Him.

There are those who have great struggles with demons on their deathbeds, usually people who treated others coldly, or even cruelly. There is shouting, tossing and turning, writhing, an anguished fear of something they see but others don't. In one case, a hospital camera even seemed to pick up a dark form hovering over a person's bed. In other cases, the dying may be taken over, thrashing.

This makes it important to find deliverance from evil while we are on earth.

"I bless the Lord Who gives me counsel; in the night also my heart instructs me," says *Psalms*. "I keep the Lord always before me; because He is at my right hand, I shall not be moved. Therefore my heart is glad, and my soul rejoices; my body also dwells secure. For Thou dost not give me up to Sheol, or let Thy Godly one see the Pit."

Chapter 21

The vast majority of people feel angels and departed loved ones around them.

The doctor I mentioned named Dr. Reggie Anderson, who has a "gift" for sensing the departure of those dying, experiences what he describes as "the veil parting—the veil that separates this life from the next. As I held a dying woman's hands, I felt the warmth of her soul pass by my cheek when it left her body, swept up by an inexplicably cool breeze in an otherwise stagnant room. I smelled the familiar fragrance of lilac and citrus, and I knew the veil was parting to allow her soul to pass through. Since that first patient, I've walked with countless others to the doorstep of Heaven and watched them enter paradise. On many occasions, as I held hands with the dying, God allowed me to peer into Heaven's entryway where I watched each patient slip into the next world. I've sensed Jesus on the other side, standing in Heaven's foyer, welcoming the dead who are made whole again. I've glimpsed surreal colors and sights and heard sounds more intense than anything I've ever experienced in this ordinary world. I've inhaled the scents of lilac, citrus, freshly carved cedar, and baking bread—more fragrant than I ever thought possible."

The challenge on earth—your challenge—is the betterment of everything you can make better.

Many describe their death experience as the most pleasant experience of their lives—a release from the confinements of the body, a freedom over the laws of nature, a flood of light, love, and grace. They were surprised at just how tremendous it was. Virtually all of them lose their fear of death.

"Unlike earth, where I was plagued by doubts and fears, in Heaven there was nothing but absolute certainty about who I was," wrote Crystal McVea. "This was a far more complete representation of my spirit and my heart and my being than was ever possible on earth, a far deeper self-awareness than the collection of hopes and fears and dreams and scars that defined me during my life. I was flooded with self-knowledge, and all the junk that cluttered my identity on earth instantly fell away, revealing, for the first time, the real me."

You will find out the "who" God created in your mother's womb, which is the person God knows and wants you to be (*Jeremiah* 1:5). We begin to learn this also when we find joy in the sacraments. We find it at Mass, when we are attentive to His Grace. The elation of peace often flows from the beads of a Rosary. The Bible materializes a portal of Heaven.

What matters is truth.

In Heaven, we know truth without speculation.

It's there, at the snap of the fingers.

It will be there on an arbored path near a cascading waterfall taller than anything we know, feeding a river that is clear beyond clear outside the cities of light which could span a continent. There will be the crystalline waters that will cleanse, that will heal, until we are as crystalline, as pure. All is purity. We bring no cares—not to Heaven. Endurance and perseverance and inner strength you will take. If you are competitive, you might as well leave that behind right now: You will not have a single grudge in this place. You will not seek to be above others. There'll be no ambition that does not serve others. There will be not one lingering regret. "Create in me a clean heart, O God, and put a new and right spirit within me," says *Psalms.*

"Cast me not away from Thy Presence, and take not Thy Holy Spirit from me. Restore to me the joy of Thy salvation."

Seek His touch, His nearness, His solace.

Lord, is my assignment done? I want to take that accomplishment with me!

Lord, let me know all I need to do, everything You expect of me.

Be joyful. It purifies.

There is every reason for it!

In Heaven we are not just aware of God but see and hear and feel Him with different senses.

"His radiance wasn't simply something I could observe," wrote McVea. "It was something that overwhelmed every sense I had. In Heaven we don't have just five senses; we have a *ton* of senses. Imagine a sense that allowed us to not only see light, but also to taste it. Imagine another sense that isn't taste or touch but some *new way* to experience something, creating a more amazing and rewarding connection than any of our earthly senses allow."

Who possibly could not want to love the Creator of this reality?

A place where roses are massive and trees a mile wide with diamond leaves and fruit that grows on lush vines and tastes like peach and honey and pear combined but bears no sticky residue, fruit that is replaced on the branch by other fruit as soon as it is picked, flowers that can be plucked to smell and then set down and that immediately regain root and continue to live in this place, as we said, where there is no rot or decay or death.

It is the place we reach when suffering has produced perseverance and perseverance has produced character and character, hope (*Romans* 5:3-4), which leads to joy. Find gladness in God and you will lessen purgatory.

Character comes with you; fortitude; courage. Oh yes: courage! It is a manifestation of faith. "Never will I leave you, never will I forsake you" (*Hebrews* 13:5-6).

Some make the passage on a "staircase." In Pilipchuk's description, "On either side of the staircase were golden railings, along which from the bottom to the top were winged angels in white clothes, with golden belts. Their hair was white, their faces shone like lightning, and their eyes were like two lanterns. Their hands and legs were the color of shiny copper chips. Around the staircase and under it stood a great number of angels; these were without wings. All the angels were singing psalms in a language I did not recognize at first. After a moment I completely understood the words of the Psalm. They sang: 'O worthy are you Lord of all glory and praise. You, Lord, created the heavens and the earth. You are worthy of our praise!' Then I saw an extraordinary light at the end of the staircase. The light wasn't like that of the sun or of a welding instrument, which has a harmful effect on the eyes. It was extremely bright, warm, calming, full of joy and peace. I was full of delight, to such an extent that mere words cannot describe how I felt. My delight continued to increase and there was no limit to the joy I felt."

Joy?

It is hope magnified.

Joy finds God Who is the kindest, nicest, most understanding "person" you have ever known, multiplied by infinity.

"The city does not need the sun or the moon to shine on it, for the glory of God gives it light, and the Lamb is its lamp," says *Revelation* 21:33.

"Thrones were set up and the Ancient One took his throne," says *Daniel* (7:9). "His clothing was bright as snow, and his hair as white as wool."

God is light and light is love and love is the light that gives life.

It makes music.

There are chimes. There are massive chimes.

There is deepest bass and the highest soprano in the fullness of sound.

Honesty?

You take this, for sure. Trueness. Honesty. Knowledge. Pretenses evaporate like fog, revealing a true landscape. Of all knowledge, none is more essential than knowing Christ.

He is the door through which we will *all* return.

Some know that now. Some learn this later.

Use the sacraments to form a personal relationship with Him.

We die with the happiness we possess. We keep our wisdom. Works of charity enter. With those we build, we soar; we go from the rustic countryside, from the chrysolite roads, from the waters that capture gold from the sky to higher elevations and then yet higher until there is more mind and spirit than even there is an illuminated celestial body; more oneness with the Lord—more proximity to the wise men in the Place of Communion (*"Isangano"*), to the Place of the Cherished, where joy is an end in itself, where our robes brighten—glisten as if we are a light that weaves through other light, an arm but not an arm, tiny sparkles, a leg but not a leg, this light that forms not just around us but our parts; a light that comes through us, that connects so completely with all the other forms of light—the interior lights, the emanating lights, the radiance from other beings—that will now be all around us.

"On the fourth dive, he suddenly saw her body," notes a passage about a drowned girl and the rescue attempts of a diver in twenty feet of water.

Approaching the girl, the diver said that to his amazement he saw her body as "illuminated from within" by a soft bright light that evoked "a sense of awe and reverence," as if viewing her spiritual part separating from the physical. It did not fully part, for she was rushed to the hospital and lived. "A few days later," said a newspaper, the diver "returned to the site with scuba gear. He wanted to see just how much natural light actually reached the bottom of Puget Sound on a sunny day. He said he could see only a few feet in front of his eyes."

Bright clouds, radiant clouds, as we are also radiant with no dark cloud within. We have no more cares. We soar on that gaiety. We think, "There is no death! *There is no death!*" The realization is as powerful as it is final. There is no more doubt, no more despair, not a bit; not the tiniest element of that. Death ceases to accompany us. There is the clarity of everlasting light driving away wrong passions with a peace that rules inside us through an abundance of glory and praise to God. The chambers of our souls are pure; we have a clean conscience. No embarrassment is "brought" because there is no such thing as embarrassment in a place where everyone knows and understands everything and the reason for it. All is explained. There is no more judgment. Home. Truth. Well-being. The air is music; grace is the breeze. "As I reached the Light, I could see in," said a man whose vital signs had vanished. "I cannot begin to describe in human terms what I saw. It was a giant world of calm, and love, and energy, and beauty."

"For me it was a time of indescribable joy and bliss, in a place and environment of exquisite harmony," said a woman named Dorothy Kerin who was in a life-ending coma back in 1912. "I seemed to drift into space. I was no longer conscious of my body, but my soul was overflowing with love and joy, and a transcendent feeling of supreme happiness, impossible to describe in ordinary language. I passed on, and as I went, the way grew brighter and brighter, until I saw in front of me a wonderful altar, formed by angels. There were six in the back, and in the front one more beautiful than the rest holding a chalice, which he brought to me and from which he gave me to drink. Then they disappeared, and as they went, they seemed to be chanting words which I could not understand."

Dorothy passed on again, according to author Tessy Rawlins, and saw robed figures coming from every direction.

It seemed like she was going back and forth between the here and the hereafter.

"No words of mine can exaggerate the exquisite beauty of the scene," she recalled; their movements made a lovely music. After passing for a third time, a voice told her, *"Dorothy, you are not coming yet."* Then a great light surrounded her and an angel took her hand, saying, *"Dorothy, your sufferings are over and you can walk."* She was healed. Her mission henceforth: "to heal the sick, and bring comfort." Later she studied theology at Saint Mark's Church in Bush Hill Park in the United Kingdom and she received the marks of Jesus (stigmata) on her body. (She was Anglican, the first on record to have those wounds. In death she found her mission, opening her first "Home of Healing" in a small house and dedicated her life to trying to heal and comfort those who came to her.)

Service. Service.

Said Kempis, "Confirm me, Lord, by the grace of the Holy Spirit, and give me grace to be strong inwardly in soul and to cast out from it all unprofitable business of the world and of the flesh, that it may not be led by unstable desires of earthly things; grant that I may behold all things in this world as they are—transitory and of short abiding. Enlighten me, Lord Jesus, with the clarity of everlasting light, and drive out of my heart all manner of darkness and all vain imaginations and violent temptation. Fight strongly for me and drive away the evil beasts—that is, all my evil and wicked [instincts]—so that peace of conscience may enter and fully rule within me, and that an abundance of glory and praise of Your Name may sound continually in the chamber of my soul in a pure and clean conscience."

This will be your raiment: your conscience. You'll wear it right into the "tunnel," right as you rise, over the "bridge," through the gates.

"Clothing was made out of heavenly material," said Sigmund. "I saw people dressed like one would think an angel would dress: long, flowing robes. I saw others of different colors. I cannot put into words how beautiful it was to see all these different people with the fabulous adornments. Nowhere did I see jewelry hanging off people. It wasn't necessary. The glow of God's Presence just makes a person beautiful. I saw the Lord and He had gold around the ends of His sleeves and around His collar. He also had a golden waist band and gold around the hem of His robe. It is the style of the clothes in Heaven."

It will be yours and you will wear it amidst the rainbow colors of flowers that spring around you and on those rolling hills above verdant valleys and the crystal trees with diamond leaves in a sea of light as through a vast prism with no limit on variations of color captured by buildings filled with aspects of God's knowledge you never imagined, this place where millions of angels go but where even after two thousand years of studying that knowledge you would have sampled only a page or two of it. The Library of God's Knowledge. The design of the universe. Your place in it—your indelible place, written there, etched, before the beginning of time, before our particular cosmos was formed; before any cosmos was formed, a universe that teems with life—is there. God forms where God will. God always creates. We will watch Him. We will assist Him. We will assist Jesus. We will run errands to far reaches beyond fascination, high above lakes that sparkle with perfection. Your intention will be solely what God intends, which will yield all the more happiness.

"A powerful aid in preserving recollection is the remembrance of the Presence of God," Saint Alphonsus advises us. "Not only does it conduce to recollection of spirit, but it is also one of the most effective means of advancing in the spiritual life; it helps us to avoid sin; it spurs us in the practice of virtue, and it brings about an intimate union of the soul with God. There is no more excellent means of quieting the passions and of resisting the temptation to sin than the thought of the Presence of God."

Saint Thomas adds, "If we thought of the Presence of God at all times we would never, or very seldom, do anything to displease Him."

According to Saint Jerome, the recollection of God's Presence closes the door on every sin.

"The cause of all evil lies in the fact," said Saint Teresa of Avila, "that we do not think of the Presence of God, but imagine Him far away from us."

By the thought of God's ever-vigilant Eye we, like saints, have strength to resist all the attacks of the evil one.

Said Saint Chrysostom: "If we keep ourselves in the Presence of God we shall neither think nor say nor do what is wrong, convinced as we are that God is the witness of all our thoughts and words and actions. It is not necessary to ascend to Heaven to find the Lord God; we need only to recollect ourselves, and we shall find Him within us. He who, at prayer, pictures the Lord at a great distance from Him is preparing for himself a source of abundant distractions."

You are a temple of the Holy Spirit and so you can go deep inside and clean everything and find Heaven even before you go there—find a way to the other side that will be such that you will not even feel the passage; the Blessed Mother promised this!

Pray enough and death will lose its sting—all of it.

Be holy.

In holiness, have joy.

Be benevolent in all things.

Let fun—Godly fun—lead the way.

Love all that God has created.

Love all life around you.

Go in the direction of happiness.

Forget pretense.

Impress Him only.

Find yourself.

In your soul is His Fingerprint.

Open your heart and answers will pour out.

"I'm happy!" you will say one day. "I'm so *happy*! I am totally and fully and completely full of happiness!"

That is your destination.

Heaven is happiness.

One day it will materialize in a way that soars beyond your dearest hopes, your most extravagant dreams.

The illusion is earth, a fraction of the infinite. Heaven is real. The Light of the Lord is the source of all. "When it ends, will my life have mattered?"

You will take this answer with you: Yes!

And before you will be angels and ancestors who will radiate, who will know you profoundly, who will love you most dearly. When you die you will learn that your life on earth was as important as anyone's.

His Love will make you feel like you are the only one.

Love God and live bravely.

It's that easy.

Murmur always, *"Jesus."*

Find in His Light an ocean of glory (and mercy).

Here on earth, just hold His lamp.

That's all: just hold it. Raise it.

Ask Him to expiate.

This will dissolve what's dark in your past.

Go forward in purity. Love, light, and purity. That's all it takes. It is when you rediscover that light that you will meld with His Place of Dwelling, that you are in His Presence—if not the highest place, if not the brightest city, if not the purest realm (right off), on your way.

Music felt. Voices pure. Each note clear. Loved ones. Each sight brilliant.

God is love and love is light and you take the brightness of your luminosity—your trueness—with you. "I am happy. I am happiest! So much joy!" you will say as you move to a place where angels orchestrate the music of the spheres, where death is never feared again, where colors shift marvelous hues, where space knows no bounds. "I am almost too filled with joy!" you will think, as you rise through forever.

Notes

I'd like to thank my wife Lisa for her proficient advice, editing, and proof-reading—crucial as always! And Judy Berlinski, for her expert formatting and proofing, along with Pete Massari for the great cover.

I have used many sources for this work: books, articles, video interviews, on-line testimonies, websites, blogs, personal e-mail communications, my own interviews, personal encounters with folks at public events, and so forth. As always, it is for our discernment. The first major figure to log near-death experiences in detail was Pope Gregory the Great. Thus, there is a Catholic underpinning. Most near-death experiences contradict nothing in Christian and Catholic dogma. However, they come from many different belief systems. I always urge folks to discern all mysticism, taking what is good, as Scripture admonishes (*1 Thessalonians* 5:21), and leaving the rest. These experiences often come through the lens of a person's own beliefs, or are given a certain "spin" afterwards, according to personal interpretations. Can there be deception? Yes. Is there goodness in many of these? Yes. The quote in Chapter Two from Seattle comes from Kenneth Ring's *Lessons from the Light*. Dr. Ring was a paramount researcher and college professor. The "groundbreaking" book mentioned is *Life After Life,* by Dr. Raymond Moody, which was published way back in 1975 and was truly a pioneering work. The quote in Chapter Three about the dark side of death is from Dr. Reggie Anderson's *Appointments with Heaven.* The quote from Karen is in *Echoes From Eternity* by Arvin S. Gibson. This was also the source for some of Elane Durham's quotes. For Kibeho see *Kibeho Rwanda: A Prophecy Fulfilled* by Father Gabriel Maindron. The quote on the doctor who glimpsed eternity and spoke about the bondage of guilt is from Dr. John Lerma's *Into the Light*. He also wrote *Learning From the Light.* The quote from Roberts Liardon is from *We Saw Heaven.* The quote from Peggy is from *Lessons from the Light.* Much of the background on the "illumination" comes from *The Miracle of the Illumination of All Consciences*, by Thomas W. Petrisko. The quotes from Bryan Melvin are from Sanctifiedchurchrevolutiuon.com and his book, *A Land Unknown.* The quotes from Dr. Gloria Polo are from her intense book, *Struck By Lightning.* I also used her audio testimony. The quotes from Marvin Besteman are from his book, *My Journey To Heaven.* The quote on colors and music are from blogs, including one operated by Daniel Lovett. The quote from Christine Eastell is from a video interview with Dr. Richard Kent; I also included short quotes from her as recorded in *HeavenVision* by Terry James. "The Seven Capital Sins" is published by Tan Publishing. The booklet *The Secrets of Purgatory* (author unknown) was published by Divine World Publications in Techny, Illinois. The quotes from Maria Simma are from *The Amazing Secrets of the Souls in Purgatory* by Sister Emmanuel (Queenship Publishing). The quote from Grace Bubulka is from *Beyond This Reality.* A quote on life reviews is from Ring's book. The quote from the member of the Knights of Columbus in Wisconsin was on YouTube. The quotes from Jedediah Grant as well as Bob Helm are from *The Eternal Journey*, by Dr. Craig R. Lundahl and Dr. Harold A. Widdison; the quotes from Rebecca Springer are from her book, *Within Heaven's Gates.* The quote from Boris Pilipchuk is from *HeavenVision.* The quote in Chapter 16 on taking illness is from Wanda Pratnicka's *Possessed By Ghosts.* Dr. George Ritchie's quotes are from his books, *Return from Tomorrow* and *Ordered to Return: My Life After Dying.* The quote from Lany Leary is from YouTube. The descriptions from Marian seers come largely from Jan Connell's excellent, *Queen of the Cosmos*, as well as Father Rene Laurentin's *Is The Virgin Mary Appearing At Medjugorje*? Saint Teresa's quotes are from her classic work, *The Life of Teresa of Jesus*. The quote from the preacher is from an interview with T. D. Jakes published in the *Christian Post*. The quote from the woman about no clock in Heaven is from *You Live Forever* by Gladys L. Hargis. The quote from Elane Durham is from *The Eternal Journey*. The quote from Hermossillo is in *Near Death Experiences: True Stories of Those Who Went to Heaven*, by Tessy Rawlins. The woman from Seattle, Betty Eadie, wrote the massive bestseller, *Embraced By the Light*, from which I draw several quotes. Quotes about spiritual warfare and some other matters are from her excellent 1999 book, *The Ripple Effect*, as is the quote from an experiencer who talks about looking skyward. The quote from Nathan is from *Near Death Experiences* (previously cited). For a discussion of various sins see *The Art of Dying Well* by Father Bellarmine and *Bathe Seven Times* by Nadine Brown. The Lani Leary quote was taken from an online video clip. A quote from a priest about such experiences is from the diocesan newspaper in Milwaukee. The Moorjani quote is from the television network CNN. Maurice Rawlings's book is *Beyond Death's Door*. Bill Wiese's book is *23 Minutes in Hell*. Reinee's quote was on a video linked to near-death.com. The quotes from Angie Fenimore are from her fascinating work, *Beyond the Darkness: My Near-Death Journey to the Edge of Hell and Back*; Dr. Rommer's book is *Blessing in Disguise—Another Side of the Near-Death Experience*. The quotes from saints are largely from *The Twelve Steps to Holiness and Salvation* from the adapted works of Saint Alphonsus Liguori (TAN Publishing). See also *Humble Thyself Before the Lord* (Paraclete), a collection of comments from saints. The case of Yong Thang is from a good resources online, Bibleprobe.com, as are several other cases, such as Rebecca in Chapter Three, Boris Pilipchuk, and Pastor Daniel Ekechukwu (whose story was recounted by David Servant; see also www.heavensfamily.org). The quote on fear is from Deborah Lipsky in *A Message of Hope*, an amazing work. The quote from Harry Hone is from *The Day I Died* by Tammy Cohen. The quote from Jules Lyons is from *The Wisdom of Near-Death Experiences* by Dr. Penny Sartori. The quote from Pilipchuk is from *HeavenVision* (previously cited). The quote from Archie Manning is from the *Orlando Sentinel.* The quote on taking knowledge to Heaven is from Raymond Moody's *The Light Beyond.* The quote on saints is from a blog in the Dallas area. Quotes from Howard Storm are from his book, *My Descent into Death.* The quote from René in New Zealand is from *The Day I Died* (previously cited). The quote from Dr. Rajiv Parti comes from *LA Weekly.* The author cited as far as the life review and thoughtlessness was Tony Bushby in *Glimpses of Life Beyond Death.* The quotes on the trapped miners come from an online writer named Ed Conrad. The quote from Trudy Harris is from *Glimpses of Heaven.* The television interview of Deborah Shambora was on *Sid Roth—It's Supernatural!* The quote from Crystal McVea is from *Waking Up in Heaven.* Richard Sigmund's book is *A Place Called Heaven.* The Stadler quote is from Christian Broadcasting Network (CBN). The Kempis quotes are from T*he Imitation of Christ.* The book *Glimpses of Eternity* is by the ground-breaking medical researcher, Dr. Raymond Moody. A fascinating book. Other works I used: *Delivered: A Death-Defying Journey into Heaven and Hell* by Tamara Laroux; *What Tom Sawyer Learned from Dying,* by Sidney Saylor Farr; *Cases of Apparitions Announcing Death* by C. W. Leadbeater; *At the Hour of Death* by Karlis Osis and Erlendur Haraldsson; *Closer to the Light: Near-Death Experiences as Evidence of the Afterlife,* by Melvin Morse; *The*

Case for Heaven by Mally Cox-Chapman; *Saved by the Angels: True stories of angels and near-death experiences,* by Glennyce S. Eckersley; *Eyewitness To Heaven*, by James Wilburn Chauncey; *The Truth in the Light*, by Dr. Peter Fenwick; *Absent From the Body*, by Don Brubaker; *One Last Hug Before I Go: The Mystery and Meaning of Deathbed Visions,* by Carla Wills-Brandon; *By the Light*, by Lionel C. Bascom and Barbara Loecher; *Glimpses Beyond Death's Door* by Brent L. and Wendy C. Top; *Possessed By Ghosts* by Wanda Pratnicka; *Life Beyond Death*, by Tony Bushby; *Angels, Miracles, and Heavenly Encounters: Real-life Stories of Supernatural Events*, compiled by James Stuart Bell; *Dying Testimonies of the Saved and Unsaved*, by S. B. Shaw; *Beyond the Veil* by Lee Nelson; *There Is Life After Death*, by Roy Abraham Varghese; *Life At Death* by Kenneth Ring.

Some in this field are labeled as New Age, and perhaps are, or put that spin on it afterward. These I disregard when I detect that—hold a distance—or take what is good and move on. Some have a touch of it: more a case of "contamination," in my discernment, than a wholesale deception. In other cases, the unusual nature of a heavenly glimpse is so different than anything we have witnessed on earth, or even read about, that we may mistakenly classify it as "New Age" when it is not. For your reckoning. My thanks to all these sincere and excellent authors, whether we agree or not.

[Note: At the apparition site of Medjugorje, Our Lady reportedly gave five wonderful promises, on September 2, 2012, for those who pray for atheists (the ones "who have not come to know the love of the Heavenly Father"). The promises are:

1. "I will strengthen you."

2. "I will fill you with my graces."

3. *"With my love, I will protect you from the evil spirit."*
4. *"I will be with you."*
5. *"With my presence, I will console you in difficult moments."*

The prayer:

"In the Name of Jesus, Who said that anything we ask in His Name will be given to those who believe, I ask that those who have not come to know the love of the Heavenly Father will be blessed with the knowledge that they are loved by Him beyond all human reasoning and understanding. Please grant them the gift to feel His love as it enfolds them to such an extent that they will be unable to resist or deny it. May the knowledge of the Heavenly Father's infinite love stir within their hearts the desire to return that love to Him, and to reflect it to all others. May their lives be a pure reflection of His resplendent love. I ask this in the Name of the Father, and the Son, and the Holy Spirit, through the Immaculate Heart of Mary. Amen"]

About the author

A former investigative reporter, Michael H. Brown, 62, is the author of twenty-six books, most of them Catholic. He has appeared on numerous TV and radio shows, and contributed to publications from *Reader's Digest* to *The Atlantic Monthly*. He is the author of the Catholic bestsellers *The Final Hour*, *The God of Miracles*, and *The Other Side*, and lives in Florida with wife Lisa and three children. He is also director of the Catholic news website, Spirit Daily (www.spiritdaily.com).

Other Books by Michael H. Brown

Available at www.spiritdaily.com

THE SPIRITS AROUND US

LIFE MISSIONS, FAMILY HEALING

THE OTHER SIDE

THE GOD OF MIRACLES

AFTER LIFE

PRAYER OF THE WARRIOS

THE FINAL HOUR